C000104201

Walking with William Shakespeare

Walking with
WILLIAM SHAKESPEARE

ANNE-MARIE EDWARDS

Photographs by Michael Edwards

JONES BOOKS
Madison, Wisconsin

Copyright © Anne-Marie Edwards 2005. All rights reserved.

Jones Books
309 N. Hillside Terrace
Madison, Wisconsin 53705-3328
www.jonesbooks.com

First edition, first printing

Library of Congress Cataloging-in-Publication Data

Edwards, Anne-Marie.
  Walking with William Shakespeare / Anne-Marie Edwards.— 1st ed.
    p. cm.
  Includes index.
  ISBN 0-9763539-0-3 (alk. paper)
  1. Shakespeare, William, 1564-1616—Homes and
haunts—England—Stratford-upon-Avon—Guidebooks. 2. Dramatists,
English—Homes and haunts—England—Stratford-upon-Avon—
Guidebooks. 3. Shakespeare, William, 1564-1616—Homes and
haunts—England—Warwickshire—Guidebooks. 4. Dramatists,
English—Homes and haunts—England—Warwickshire—Guidebooks.
5. Dramatists, English—Early modern, 1500-1700—Biography.
6. Walking—England—Stratford-upon-Avon—Guidebooks.
7. Walking—England—Warwickshire—Guidebooks. 8. Stratford-upon-
Avon (England)—Guidebooks. 9. Warwickshire (England)—
Guidebooks. I.
Title.
  PR2916.E34 2005
  822.3'3—dc22
                                        2005001854

Printed in the U.S.A.

Front cover: Anne Hathaway's Cottage at Shottery, near Stratford. Photo
by Michael Edwards, courtesy of the Shakespeare Birthplace Trust.

TABLE OF CONTENTS

LIST OF
ILLUSTRATIONS

ACKNOWLEDGEMENTS

I would like to thank all those who have helped me to make this book: the staff of my local library in Totton; Bill Turner, a chapelwarden at St. Marks Woodmancote, and Sheila Wright, who also helped us in Dursley; and all the excellent guides at the Shakespeare Properties in Stratford who patiently answered my endless questions. I am grateful also to David Gajadharsingh, deputy head of King Edward VI Grammar School, Stratford, for his kindness in showing us round the school and Guild Chapel, and David Evans-Turner, BEM, who gave up so much of his time to talk to us about the Middle Temple Hall and the history of the Inns of Court. It is a real pleasure to thank David Payne, Visitors' Officer at Southwark Cathedral, for the warm welcome and valuable information he gave me, and Tony Thomas for his equally warm welcome to St. Helen's Church in Bishopsgate.

Photographs of the interior of Shakespeare's schoolroom were taken by kind permission of the King Edward VI Grammar School, Stratford, and those of Shakespeare's grave and memorial by kind permission of Holy Trinity Church, Stratford. Photographs of Southwark Cathedral were taken with the kind permission of the Dean and Chapter of Southwark, and of the interior of Middle Temple Hall by permission of the Masters of the Bench of the Honourable Society of the Middle Temple. I am grateful to the Shakespeare Birthplace Trust for allowing me to reproduce photographs of Anne Hathaway's Cottage, Mary Arden's House, and Hall's Croft taken from the gardens. The photograph of the interior of Shakespeare's Globe was taken by kind permission of the theater, and the photograph of the George Inn, Southwark, by kind permission of the National Trust.

I thank all my friends for their help and encouragement, especially Sybil Lines, an experienced actress who has spent some time with the Royal Shakespeare Company. She gave me valuable insights into Shakespeare's work and made many helpful suggestions. My thanks also to Maisie Bailey for help with the Titchfield chapter, Martin and Clare Tate, who guided me in the ways of computers, Dick and Liz Snell for their cheerful encouragement, and Jack and Johanna Jones for their suggestions. I am grateful to my publisher, Joan Strasbaugh, for her enthusiastic support, Janet Trembley, who designed the book, and Carrie Bebris, who so painstakingly edited the text. Finally, I thank our daughter, Julie, for her unfailing support and my husband, Mike, who, while performing wonders with map and compass, manages to take the photographs as well. He was with me every step of the way, and without him this book would never have been written.

INTRODUCTION

All the world's a stage,
And all the men and women merely players:
They have their exits and their entrances;
And one man in his time plays many parts. . . .
—Jaques, *As You Like It*

No writer in the English language has portrayed our humanity, as we play our parts on the world's great stage, with deeper sympathy and understanding than William Shakespeare. His ability to see life whole, to question why we behave as we do, makes his work as relevant today as it was during the reign of Queen Elizabeth I. As his friend and rival Ben Jonson wrote, "He was not of an age, but for all time!" Yet in spite of the huge library of books his work has inspired, for many of us he remains strangely remote. So often he features as someone we "do" at school as a necessary part of an exam syllabus, and the delight we should experience in his knowledge of life and in the beauty and music of his poetry is lost as we struggle with the unfamiliar world of the Elizabethans and their stage. The aim of this book is to help to make this most rewarding of writers more approachable by walking, quite literally, in his footsteps.

Although London necessarily claimed so much of his life, Shakespeare remained devoted to his native Warwickshire and the small market town of Stratford-upon-Avon where he was born in 1564. Warwickshire is a small diamond-shaped county in the Midlands—the middle of the country, often called "the Heart of England." It is bordered to the south and east by the Northamptonshire and Oxfordshire hills and to the west by the woodlands of Worcestershire. Stratford is tucked comfortably in the southwest of the county beside the river Avon with an outlook over the Vale of the Red Horse to the Cotswold Hills. Surrounding the little market town is countryside often felt to be typically "English," a world of half-timbered houses, quiet riverside paths and flower-bordered lanes. The charm of this lovely scenery has been immortalized by Shakespeare in his plays. He is sensitive to the tiniest detail, noting the freckles in a cowslip's bell and the wren's upright "little quill." As we walk with him, we can enjoy his images of country life and share his delight in nature.

Few traces remain of the great Forest of Arden, the home of the exiled duke in *As You Like It* and the quarrelsome fairies in *A Midsummer Night's Dream*, that in Shakespeare's day lay north of Stratford. But the forest villages where his parents were born and the churches where family marriages took place remain much as he knew them. South of the town, beyond the Avon, lay a rich area of open fields known as the Feldon. Although it is now enclosed and more thickly hedged, it is still recognizable today.

As the eldest son, Shakespeare often visited the Cotswold Hills with his wool-trading father, and he knew the area well. The Cotswolds are a particularly beautiful part of England, with Old World villages built of honey-colored stone nestling in the valleys. Since medieval days, sheep have thrived on the rich grass of the chalk downland, producing fine quality wool. The delightful sheep-shearing feast in *The Winter's Tale* is among many scenes Shakespeare set in these hills. Against a realistically earthy picture of country life, Perdita, the queen of the feast, welcomes her handsome prince in some of Shakespeare's most exquisite poetry. But life in the Warwickshire countryside, and in Stratford, also had its more somber side, and Shakespeare depicts humanity in its entirety. We meet rogues and vagabonds as well as shepherds. In the same play, the pickpocket Autolycus roams the countryside with his pedlar's pack, preying on the gullibility of the simple village folk.

The exact date when Shakespeare left Stratford for London is not known, but it is likely that he joined the Queen's Players when they visited Stratford in 1587 and returned to London with them as a "hired man" capable of acting small parts and revising old plays as well as contributing his own scripts. He must have been stunned by the contrast between his native countryside and the teeming metropolis with a population of over 200,000, its narrow streets pulsing with life. A glittering court revolved around a much-loved queen, music filled the air, and huge crowds thronged the inn yards and theatres to hear plays written in the new rhythmical medium of blank verse. Outstanding among the playwrights was Christopher Marlowe, whose "mighty line" was holding audiences spellbound as Shakespeare arrived. But the same crowd would also rush to witness the appalling public executions at Tyburn and the bear- and bull-baiting across the river in Southwark. Beauty and brutality existed side by side, a paradox which Shakespeare recognized and questioned. In one of his sonnets, he writes:

How 'gainst this rage shall beauty hold a plea
Whose action is no stronger than a flower?

John Aubrey, writing *Brief Lives* in the mid-seventeenth century, obtained some of his information for his biography of Shakespeare from Christopher Beeston, the son of William Beeston, one of the playwright's fellow actors. He describes Shakespeare as "a handsome well shap't man: very good company, and of a very readie and pleasant smooth wit." The London stage offered Shakespeare a golden opportunity to use his talents and earn an income. Here he found the inspiration for his plays and an audience to approve them. Surrounded by the racy, low life of the streets, he wrote his comedies—out of the London taverns emerged the immensely popular figure of Falstaff. But at the same time, the suffering and corruption he witnessed led him to question human weakness in the face of evil and produce his great tragedies. We explore some of the London he knew and the areas where he took lodgings north of the Thames. Then we cross the river to Bankside in Southwark, in his day a disreputable area and the center of all amusements. We discover the site of his famous Globe Theatre (the "wooden O" of *Henry V*) and visit the splendid new Globe that shares the same setting overlooking the river to St. Paul's Cathedral.

Shakespeare lodged and made his fortune in London, but every year he returned home to Stratford, where he invested his money in land and property. We return with him to walk in the Welcombe Hills just north of town, where he bought land in 1602. Some of his later plays, romances notable for their gentle themes of forgiveness and reconciliation, were possibly written in the serene atmosphere of his comfortable Stratford home, New Place. We take a final walk with him beside the river Avon, where he had swum and fished as a boy, and visit Holy

Trinity Church, where, after his death on April 23, 1616, he was buried.

The tours in this book are easy walking and demand no special equipment apart from strong, comfortable footwear. All the routes are circular and vary in length between 3 and 6 miles. The sketch maps accompanying each walk are designed to guide you to the start and give an overall picture of the route. For more detailed information, arm yourself with the relevant Ordnance Survey® Explorer™ map—at a scale of 1:25,000 (2.5 inches to 1 mile), ideal for walkers—mentioned in the notes just before each "Walk in Brief" summary. Each walk includes information on how to get to the start and where to park. All the starting points are accessible by public transport, so there is no problem if you have to rely on buses. The starting point for each walk is indicated by a Grid Reference—the letters GR followed by two groups of numbers. This code refers to the National Grid Reference System of numbered horizontal and vertical lines that overlay the Ordnance Survey (OS®) maps and make it possible to locate with reasonable accuracy anywhere you wish to find. The system and how to use it is explained in full under the "General Information" heading on the maps. If you are unfamiliar with the English countryside, you may find it helpful to read the "Walking in England" chapter at the end of this book for some useful tips before setting out.

Shakespeare's language is rich and expressive but at times can be difficult to follow. Spelling in his day could be erratic, and even his contemporaries would have been puzzled by some of the words he used, as he was coining them as he wrote! When I felt it would be helpful, I have modernized Elizabethan spelling and typography and added a gloss in square brackets. Longer passages of verse are separated from the text, but short citations appear in quotation marks. A slash (/) indicates the beginning of a new line. After the first heading, I have abbreviated Stratford-upon-Avon to Stratford.

I have found writing this book both rewarding and challenging. There are very few documented facts concerning Shakespeare's life; books about him tend to be personal interpretations based on his plays or comments made by his contemporaries and early biographers. These sources can be more or less trustworthy depending on the character of the speaker. In his delightful life of the poet, Ivor Brown remarks, "All excursions in discovery of Shakespeare are essays in conjecture and anyone may compete." This must be my excuse if, as you walk with me, you find me straying too often into the world of mere supposition!

Finally, I wish you many happy hours walking with William Shakespeare.

Anne-Marie Edwards
Ashurst, New Forest
England

CALENDAR

1534	Henry VIII declared himself supreme head of the Church in England
1535	Publication of Miles Coverdale's first complete Bible in English
1536–1539	Dissolution of the monasteries and religious houses. The Great Bible was placed in every parish church. (Shakespeare was strongly influenced by the Bible, especially the psalms.)
1542	William Byrd founded the English Madrigal School. (Music and song are important in Shakespeare's plays.)
1553	Performance of Nicholas Udall's *Ralph Roister Doister*, the earliest English comedy. Accession to the throne of Catholic Mary Tudor
1555	Persecution of Protestants
1557	Publication of *Songes and Sonettes* (*Tottel's Miscellany*)
1558	Accession of Protestant Elizabeth I (She enjoyed plays and supported the theatre; Shakespeare's plays were performed in her palaces as well as the playhouses)
1559	Acts of Supremacy and Uniformity restored

	the Protestant Church
1561	Performance of Sackville and Norton's *Gorboduc, or Ferrex and Porrex*, the first play in blank verse
1567	Arthur Golding translated Ovid's *Metamorphoses* into English verse (Ovid was Shakespeare's favorite classical author and there are many references to Ovid in his plays; he probably consulted Golding's translation for speed)
1570	Elizabeth was excommunicated by Pope Pius V; increased persecution of recusants (those who refused to attend church and receive Protestant Communion)
1576	James Burbage opened the first purpose-built playhouse in England in London's Shoreditch; he called it the Theatre
1579	Sir Thomas North translated Plutarch's *Lives* from the French (Shakespeare used Plutarch as a source for some of his plays.)
1583	Elizabeth ordered a group of players to be assembled under her patronage, to be known as the Queen's Men
1587	Execution of Mary Queen of Scots. Christopher Marlowe's blank verse tragedies *Tamburlaine* and *Faustus*
1588	Defeat of the Armada
1590	Marlowe's *The Jew of Malta*
1592	Plague closed playhouses
1593	Playhouses still closed. Death of Marlowe. Shakespeare wrote his poem *Venus and Adonis*, followed by *The Rape of Lucrece*, both dedicated to the young Earl of Southampton. Much alteration of players' companies
1594	Formation of the Lord Chamberlain's Men

(Shakespeare was a prominent member and remained with them.) Highly successful performance of Thomas Kyd's bloodthirsty tragedy *The Spanish Tragedy* (This could have led Shakespeare to write his equally bloodthirsty *Titus Andronicus*.)

1599	Building of the Globe theater by Richard Burbage and the Lord Chamberlain's Men
1601	Insurrection and execution of the Earl of Essex
1603	Death of Elizabeth and accession of James I, a strong supporter of the theater. The Lord Chamberlain's Men became the King's Men and wore his livery
1605	Discovery of the Gunpowder Plot
1608	The King's Men took over the roofed Blackfriars theater in a fashionable area of London. Performance of Ben Jonson's *Volpone* and *The Alchemist*. Jonson and Inigo Jones became popular producing masques: light entertainments combining dialogue, song, and spectacular stage effects
1609	Publication of Shakespeare's sonnets
1612	Death of Henry, Prince of Wales
1615	Inigo Jones became England's chief architect, bringing the Renaissance style in building to England
1623	The First Folio edition of Shakespeare's plays was published by two of his friends and fellow actors, John Heminge and Henry Condell.

1564	William Shakespeare was born on or around April 23. He was christened in Stratford's Holy Trinity Church on the 25th. He was the third child of John and Mary Shakespeare. Stratford town records mention his father trading as a glover from two houses in Henley Street. But both John and Mary were descended from old yeoman families with farmsteads in the villages close to Stratford in the Forest of Arden. Shakespeare's plays are full of references to country sports, flowers and animals.
1568	After holding several important posts in the town, John Shakespeare was elected bailiff (mayor).
1571	As a burgess, John was entitled to send William to the town's free grammar school, which the boy attended from the age of seven. He would already have learned to read and write at the petty school held in the Guild Chapel. Although early records of the school have not survived, it is clear from the evidence in his plays that he received a typical Tudor grammar school education based on Latin and classical authors. A great deal of memorizing was involved, but schooling did have its lighter moments. Boys were encouraged to give speeches, take part in debates, and act plays.
1576–1596	John Shakespeare's fortunes declined. He lost his position as alderman, was forced to sell and mortgage property, and in 1582 was included in a list of recusants "for not comminge monethlie to churche." He pleaded fear of being arrested for debt. Owing

to these difficult family circumstances, William left school early, possibly before he was sixteen. Soon he was courting Anne Hathaway of nearby Shottery.

1582   Anne became pregnant. She was the daughter of a respectable family and a hasty marriage was necessary. On November 27 an entry in the Bishop of Worcester's register recorded the issue of a special license for the marriage, as there was only time for the banns to be called once. The marriage to Anne Hathaway took place, possibly on November 30. No church records mention the marriage, but I believe it probably took place at Temple Grafton. Shakespeare was eighteen; Anne was twenty-six.

1583   In May their first child was born and christened Susanna.

1585   Twins, christened Hamnet and Judith, were born.

The years between 1585 and the recorded presence of Shakespeare in London in 1592 are often called "the lost years," as nothing is known for certain. An early biographer, John Aubrey, states that in his younger days Shakespeare spent some time as a schoolmaster in the country. There is a tradition that this could have been at Dursley, an old market town at the foot of the Cotswold escarpment, an area Shakespeare knew well and features in his plays.

1587   Most authorities agree that Shakespeare left Stratford for London about this time, possibly joining the Queen's Men. This may have caused consternation in the Shakespeare household, as actors, unless they could obtain patronage, were considered vagabonds.

1592   Robert Greene, an embittered writer, attacked Shakespeare, now presumably a successful playwright, in a pamphlet called *Greene's Groats-worth of Wit*. Later in the year, the printer, Henry Chettle, prompted by protests from influential people, published a fulsome apology praising Shakespeare.

1593   In this plague year, the playhouses were closed, and Shakespeare needed the support of a patron. He chose a brilliant and handsome young man, Henry Wriothesley, third Earl of Southampton and Baron of Titchfield. He dedicated a long poem, *Venus and Adonis*, to the earl, which was an immediate success. Dedicating his next poem, *The Rape of Lucrece*, to the earl, Shakespeare wrote he was "assured of its acceptance." This was the beginning of a difficult and unequal friendship. The young earl, an only son and fatherless, needed to marry to ensure an heir. Possibly encouraged by Southampton's mother, Shakespeare wrote a sequence of sonnets urging the young man to marry. The later sonnets, chronicling the deepening friendship with Southampton and the love triangle that developed with a mysterious "dark lady," were probably written before 1598, as in that year Francis Meres mentions that they were being read in private by his friends. (Some authorities believe that William Herbert, Earl of Pembroke, was "the lovely boy" to whom the sonnets were addressed. I find this unlikely [see chapter 7]. To support this claim, the sonnets would have to have been written later, as Pembroke was only fifteen in 1595.)

1595   Shakespeare, Richard Burbage, and Will Kemp, "servants to the lord Chamberlain," were named in a document as payees for court performances on December 26 and 28. Shakespeare was now an important member of the company.

1596   In August, Shakespeare's son, Hamnet, died and was buried at Stratford. A darker mood entered his plays, and the great tragedies were to follow. But his success in the theater had restored the family fortunes, and in October Shakespeare went to the College of Arms in London to apply for the status of gentleman for his father. At the height of his prosperity, his father had applied for gentleman status and failed. His influential son was successful and the motto on his father's coat of arms read "Non Sanz Droict"—Not Without Right.
        James Burbage bought the Great Parliament Chamber, once part of Blackfriars Priory, and converted it into a theater. Local protests prevented him from using it.

1597   Shakespeare bought one of the finest houses in Stratford, New Place.

1598   In December, faced with problems over the tenancy of the Theatre in Shoreditch, the Burbage family, helped by an experienced carpenter, dismantled the building. They carried the sections over the frozen Thames

	and assembled a new theater, to be called the Globe, on a site they leased on Bankside in Southwark.
1599	Shakespeare became one of the original housekeepers of the Globe, with a one-tenth share. He was now deriving income as the company's principal playwright, from acting, and from theater receipts. Our greatest poet was also a shrewd businessman!
1600	Blackfriars was leased to Henry Evans and Nathaniel Giles for performances by the Children of the Chapel.
1601	In September, Shakespeare's father died.
1602	Shakespeare bought 127 acres of land in Old Stratford and a cottage opposite New Place.
1603	King James I "licences and authorizes" the Lord Chamberlain's Men company, now renamed the King's Men. Acting had become a respectable occupation.
1605	Shakespeare bought the lease of part of the corn and hay tithes of Welcombe, Old Stratford, and Bishopton.
1607	Susanna married the local doctor, John Hall.
1608	The Halls' daughter, Elizabeth, was christened.
	The King's Men regained the lease for Blackfriars and, his father having died, Richard Burbage formed a company of shareholders that included Shakespeare.
1609	In September, Shakespeare's mother died. Thomas Thorpe printed Shakespeare's sonnets, dedicated to a "Mr W. H." whose identity remains a source of debate (see chapter 7). I believe he was Sir William Harvey, who married Southampton's mother

Walking with William Shakespeare

in 1598.

1610   About this time Shakespeare probably settled at Stratford in New Place.

1613   Shakespeare bought the gatehouse of the former Blackfriars Priory, close to the Blackfriars Theatre. The Globe burned down during a performance of *Henry VIII* but was quickly rebuilt.

1616   In February, Shakespeare's daughter Judith married Thomas Quiney, a vintner.
On April 23, Shakespeare died and was buried in Holy Trinity Church in Stratford two days later.

CHAPTER 1

THE SHAKESPEARES
OF ARDEN

Sweet are the uses of adversity,
Which, like the toad, ugly and venomous,
Wears yet a precious jewel in his head;
And this our life, exempt from public haunt,
Finds tongues in trees, books in the running brooks,
Sermons in stones, and good in every thing.
—Duke Senior, *As You Like It*

A s *You Like It*, one of Shakespeare's most delightful comedies, is set in the Forest of Arden, a vast area lying to the north and west of Stratford. Today only small remnants of woodland remain, but in Shakespeare's time it was richly clad in trees and dotted with villages, farms, and the isolated houses of minor gentry. The forest was only a short walk from Shakespeare's home in Henley Street, and he never lost his love of his early surroundings. When he wrote *As You Like It*, probably around 1600, Shakespeare was a successful playwright and actor living and working in London. But at heart he remained a countryman, returning to Stratford every year. A few years before the play's performance, he had bought one of the finest houses in the town, New Place, not far from the house where he was born in 1564 and the fields and woods where he had roamed as a boy. Although he was caught up in the bustling life of the great city, the sights and sounds of the Forest of Arden remained vividly present in his imagination.

Arden was in Shakespeare's blood. Both his parents, John and Mary, came from forest villages and had possibly known each other from childhood. In the 1520s, John's father, Richard Shakespeare, had left his family roots around Wroxhall (north of Warwick) and leased a house and about 80 acres of land at Snitterfield, a small village about five miles north of Stratford. His landlord was Robert Arden, a prosperous farmer living at Wilmcote, a hamlet a few miles west of the town. Robert farmed about 135 acres and another 60 acres, called Asbies, near his home. Part of Asbies included a paddock opposite his farm and a cottage built at the same time as his house, in 1514. John Shakespeare was even more enterprising than his father. He realized that town life offered more opportunities for making money than the countryside, particularly for those engaged in trade. So, probably around 1550, he left the

Sheep still graze in the meadow below the site of Richard Shakespeare's farm on the corner of Bell Lane in Snitterfield.

Snitterfield farm to apprentice himself to a glover in Stratford. It is likely he rode over the fields to Wilmcote to woo and win Robert's daughter Mary at the completion of his apprenticeship in 1557.

William Shakespeare never knew his paternal grandfather, Richard, as he died in late 1560 or early 1561, four years before William was born. But John's brother Henry continued to farm at Snitterfield on land his father had leased in the village from a manor belonging to the Hales family. Henry remained a farmer until his death in 1596. He gained a reputation as the black sheep of the family, perhaps because he was thrown out of the church for refusing to pay his tithes (part of one's income claimed by the church). Young William must often have visited his Uncle Henry and Aunt Margaret. Perhaps he helped with farm work. His plays reveal that he knew all about the need to care for the land and keep down weeds. In *Henry V*, the Duke of Burgundy compares the ravages of war in

France to neglected land:

> The even mead, that erst brought sweetly forth
> The freckled cowslip, burnet, and green clover,
> Wanting the scythe, all uncorrected, rank,
> Conceives by idleness, and nothing teems
> But hateful docks, rough thistles, kecksies, burs . . .

Among many references to the weather, so important for farmers, we find Don Pedro questioning his sad companion in *Much Ado About Nothing*:

> Why what's the matter
> That you have such a February face,
> So full of frost, of storm, and cloudiness?

No doubt William Shakespeare's father talked to him about his early days in the Forest of Arden and possibly shared with him his interest in plants and wildlife.

In *As You Like It*, Arden is partly depicted as the traditional forest of romance where it would come as no surprise to find a lioness behind a bush and palms and olive trees flourishing among the oaks. But sensitive though Shakespeare was to the old tales, in this play he depicts Arden as a real place, a recognizable English forest with typical English weather. Duke Senior, banished by his younger brother, Frederick, and compelled to seek refuge with his followers in the forest, must suffer "the churlish chiding of the winter's wind." Their lives as outcasts are difficult; they must hunt the deer for food, not pleasure.

The forest surroundings allow Shakespeare to introduce his favorite imagery, using small details drawn directly from nature. When Duke Senior's daughter, Rosalind, is also banished, she and her friend Celia find their way into the forest. Celia discovers the love-sick

Orlando "under a tree, like a dropped acorn." Shakespeare also drew a great deal of his imagery from everyday life, and *As You Like It* contains some charming instances. Rosalind tells Orlando that men must beware a woman's wiles: "make the doors upon a woman's wit, and it will fly out at a casement; shut that, and 'twill out at the key-hole; stop that, 'twill fly with the smoke out at the chimney."

One of Shakespeare's greatest strengths lies in his ability to maintain a balanced viewpoint, wherever his own sympathies may lie. He allows his people to react in their own way to each other and their surroundings. A shepherd, Corin, describes the simple hardworking life he leads in the forest: "I earn that I eat, get that I wear, owe no man hate, envy no man's happiness, glad of other men's good, content with my own; and the greatest of my pride is to see my ewes graze and my lambs suck." This could be Shakespeare's grandfather or uncle Henry speaking! But the forest, like everywhere else, has its share of unlikeable people. Phebe, a shepherdess, mocks and taunts her devoted lover, Silvius, so spitefully that Rosalind grows angry upon overhearing her. "Down on your knees," she commands Phebe, "And thank heaven, fasting, for a good man's love."

Although the Duke and most of the other fugitives in the play find comfort and peace in their new surroundings, not everyone is so happy. Touchstone, the Duke's fool (in Shakespeare's day, fools were licensed comedians employed to amuse and entertain their lords with their wit) is quick to let us know how much he dislikes the forest, commenting sourly, "Ay, now I am in Arden; the more fool I." One of the Duke's attendants, Jaques, finds his unaccustomed solitude ideal for indulging in melancholy, one of the "humours" fashionable among the aristocracy at that time. This involved him in deep reflection on the life he must now lead. Saddened by the sight of a wounded stag deserted by his fellows, he compares the animal's suffering to that of a poor man deserted by his friends:

> Sweep on you fat and greasy citizens;
> 'Tis just the fashion; wherefore do you look
> Upon that poor and broken bankrupt there?

As You Like It is a comedy with a happy ending, but like all Shakeseare's plays, it reveals the depth of his sympathy with all humanity, rich and poor. Shakespeare loved the natural beauty of his native Warwickshire, but he had seen the wretched lives of the poor in the teeming plague-haunted streets of London and witnessed the very different stresses of the wealthy—the jealousies and quarrels and power-seeking at court. The breadth of Shakespeare's experience helps to account for the unfailing popularity of his plays. In *As You Like It*, he presents another world, a place where it is possible to enjoy a simple life close to nature. Duke Senior, who has suffered betrayal in the corridors of power, compares his previous life in court with the life he now leads in the woods:

> Now my co-mates and brothers in exile,
> Hath not old custom made this life more sweet
> Than that of painted pomp? Are not these woods
> More free from peril that the envious court?

Although all Shakespeare's fugitives are happy to return to their former lives, used as they are to wealth and society—as Shakespeare knew they would be—there can be no doubt of his own feelings about Arden. The great forest was part of the countryside he loved.

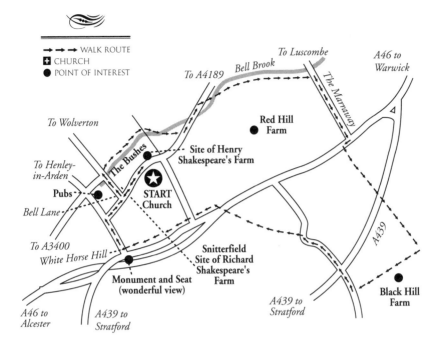

→ → → WALK ROUTE
🗧 CHURCH
● POINT OF INTEREST

To Luscombe

A46 to
Warwick

Bell Brook

To A4189

The Marraway

To Wolverton

Red Hill
Farm

The Bushes

To Henley-
in-Arden

Site of Henry
Shakespeare's Farm

Pubs

**START
Church**

Bell Lane

To A3400
White Horse Hill

Snitterfield
Site of Richard
Shakespeare's
Farm

A439

Monument and Seat
(wonderful view)

Black Hill
Farm

A46 to
Alcester

A439 to
Stratford

A439 to
Stratford

F or our first walk, we follow young William
Shakespeare to **Arden,** on a visit to his uncle's farm
at Snitterfield. His father, John, would have pointed
out to him the other farm in the village where he grew up
and the fields where he led his ox teams. We can see the
sites of both farms in this attractive village and follow field
paths Shakespeare must have known. The climax of the
walk is the marvellous view from White Horse Hill south
of the village, a view he must have enjoyed many times.
Like him, you will see the Warwickshire plain spread at
your feet, with the Cotswold Hills a faint blue smudge on
the horizon.

We start the walk from the **Church of St. James the
Great** in Church Street, the oldest part of the village.

Henry Shakespeare's farm was close by. Henry and his father, Richard, are buried in the churchyard in unmarked graves. Externally, the medieval church remains much as they would have known it. The interior has changed with the centuries, but in the chancel you will find a range of fifteenth-century panelled choir stalls carved with small figures of angels holding musical instruments, and in the south aisle a remarkable fourteenth-century font surrounded by carved heads with interesting expressions. The date of the first baptism entry in the surviving church register is January 1561, many years later than any possible dates for the births of John and Henry Shakespeare, but they were surely baptized here.

Leaving the church on your left, walk along Church Street until you come to Bell Lane. The Victorian house on the corner stands on the site of **Richard Shakespeare's farm** and is built around part of a Tudor farmhouse. Turn right to walk down Bell Lane. Sheep still graze the grassy meadows sloping down to the Bell Brook on your right—a scene which can have changed little with the centuries. Cross the bridge and follow the footpath sign on your right along Brookside. After a few yards, when the tarmac ceases, keep ahead along the path with the brook on your right. Go through the small gate and continue beside the brook along the foot of the meadow. Although the large open fields of Shakespeare's time are now smaller and hedged, the path continues through an area of tangled woodland that Shakespeare would recognize. In his day, these damp woods around the brook, now known as the Bushes, were famous for snipe, a bird that gave its name to the village. Through the trees on the right you will glimpse a rush-bordered lake.

Go through a gate and keep ahead along the narrow path past the lake. After going through another gate, cross a concrete bridge to a track. Bear right to cross the brook, then turn immediately left to keep heading east with the brook now on your left. The path narrows as it runs through bushes to a lane. Turn left along the road and walk about 150 yards to a footpath sign on the right. Turn right through a gate, then bear left along the narrow path with the Bell Brook running through a deep gully on your right. Continue through two gates, then turn right over an iron-railed bridge.

Once over the bridge, turn left and continue ahead with the brook on your left and a hedge on your right. Over the fields on your right you will see **Red Hill Farm.** Henry Shakespeare farmed land in this area. Just before he died in 1596, he was fined "for having a ditch between Red Hill and Burman in decay for want of repairing."

Cross a stile and walk over the field, still keeping the brook on your left, to go through a gate to a lane. This is an ancient road, the Marraway, which runs south to an old crossing over the Avon at Hampton Lucy. Turn right to follow the Marraway uphill to the main road, the A46. Across the road and a few yards to your right, you will see your way marked by a footpath sign. Cross the road and follow the sign through a gate. Bear left, then keep to the track as it curves right up a field to meet another main road, the A439. Cross the road and take the footpath about 30 yards to your right. The path leads you downhill with a hedge on your left. At the foot of the field is a post with several footpath signs. Turn right, with a hedge on your left, and walk ahead to a wide gap in the hedge opening to the gravelled drive to Black Hill Farm. Follow the drive, keeping the same heading, to meet a lane. It is worth pausing for a moment to enjoy a beautiful view over the leafy Warwickshire countryside. Turn right to the A439. Cross straight over and follow the lane ahead for about a

The Memorial Seat atop White Horse Hill is inscribed with a quotation from Shakespeare's King John.

quarter of a mile.

Just to the left of a long brick wall you will see a stile and footpath sign. Cross the stile and follow a raised path beside a meadow, with a garden on your right. Go through a patch of scrub to a large field. *Navigate carefully here!* The right-of-way runs half-left across the field (in the direction indicated by the footpath arrow). If you look over the field you will see the tower of Snitterfield church on the horizon a little to the right of your line of travel. Go through a gate and cross the A46 to a cycleway sign. Follow the narrow concrete path that swings left. Continue over the end of Park Lane and keep ahead up King's Lane. It is believed that King Charles II came this way as he fled from Cromwell's troops after his defeat at the battle of Worcester in 1651.

Walking with William Shakespeare

When you reach the top of **White Horse Hill,** on your left you will see the village **War Memorial**—a tall cross standing on a slight rise. It bears a simple silver sword, and the names of the many villagers who died in both world wars are inscribed round the base. In front of the cross there is a Memorial Seat where you can enjoy the wonderful view that must have delighted Shakespeare. Appropriately, the inscription on the seat refers to a quotation from one of his plays, *King John*:

> The Noble Expanse visible from this spot was Shakespeare's favourite countryside—the men whose names are inscribed on the neighbouring monument gave their lives for that England "which never did and never shall lie at the proud foot of a conqueror."

Turn right down White Horse Hill. Turn right again along Church Road to return to your starting point by the church, or continue straight ahead to the crossroads, bus stop and pubs.

Shakespeare's view over his favorite countryside from the top of White Horse Hill

Starting point
Snitterfield is about five miles north of Stratford; follow the signs for the village from the A46 or the A439. GR 218 600.

Parking
By the church in Church Street or, if there is no room, on quiet roadsides near the crossroads by the village pubs.

Public transport
Bus service from Stratford, Warwick, Leamington, Kenilworth and Coventry; for details, telephone Traveline at (0870) 608 2 608.

Length of walk: 4.5 miles.

Maps
Ordnance Survey Explorer Maps Nos. 205 and 221.

Refreshments
Snitterfield has two pubs close together, The Foxhunter and The Snitterfield Arms. The village shop sells provisions for a picnic.

THE WALK IN BRIEF

L eave the church on left and follow Church Street to the corner of Bell Lane. Turn right, cross the Bell Brook. Turn right and follow the path to a track. Turn right over the brook, then left to resume your former heading (the brook now on your left) to a lane. Turn left to a footpath sign on your right. Turn right, then immediately left to a bridge over the brook. Turn right over the bridge. Bear left, with the brook on your left, and continue to a lane, the Marraway. Turn right uphill to cross the A46. Cross, and follow the footpath sign a little to your right. Bear left, then follow the track as it curves right to the A439. Cross and follow the footpath sign posted a few yards to your right to maintain the same heading. At the marked post, turn right to the drive to Black Hill Farm. Follow the drive to a lane and turn right to the A439. Cross and follow the lane ahead for about a quarter mile. Cross the stile to the left of a long brick wall, and follow the meadow path through a patch of scrub to a large field. *Navigate carefully here!* The path bears half-left over the field—in the direction indicated by the yellow arrow footpath sign—to meet the A46. Cross the A46, take the cycleway over the foot of Park Lane, and continue up King's Lane to the top of White Horse Hill. The monument is on your left. Turn right down White Horse Hill and right again along Church Road to return to the church.

CHAPTER 2

WILMCOTE AND "A WOOD NEAR ATHENS"

I know a bank where the wild thyme blows,
Where oxlips and the nodding violet grows;
Quite over-canopied with lush woodbine,
With sweet musk-roses, and with eglantine;
There sleeps Titania sometime of the night.
—Oberon, *A Midsummer Night's Dream*

In *A Midsummer Night's Dream*, Oberon and Titania are king and queen of the fairies, and for one magical moonlit night, Shakespeare transports us into their world. Quarrelling bitterly over the possession of a changeling boy, they have come to "a wood near Athens" to celebrate the wedding of Duke Theseus and Hippolyta, the Queen of the Amazons. We have, of course, returned to Arden, where, as this is a comedy with a happy ending, all problems will soon be solved. But now Arden is an enchanted forest, a fairyland ruled by Oberon.

Shakespeare's fairies are his own creation. They are airy spirits—real, with human emotions, but of infinitesimal size. When Oberon and Titania meet and quarrel, "their elves, for fear, / Creep into acorn cups, and hide them there." All that is dainty and beautiful in nature is at their command. They also have power over the human world, and the royal bickering is causing a series of disasters. Rivers have overflowed, "rheumatic diseases do abound," even the seasons are altered: "hoary-headed frosts / Fall in the fresh lap of the crimson rose." With the forest under the spell of the fairies, it might have been wiser for humans to seek shelter elsewhere! But into the forest come two lovers, Lysander and Hermia, fleeing from a father who wishes her to marry his choice of a husband, Demetrius. They disclose their intentions to Demetrius's former love, Helena. She tells Demetrius their plans and he pursues Hermia and Lysander into the forest, followed by Helena, who still adores him. With the help of some magical love juice, Oberon is eventually able to solve both his problems and theirs—but not before a great deal of confusion. Shakespeare knew the value of laughter and weaves some humorous scenes into most of his plays. *A Midsummer Night's Dream* contains a hilarious subplot. The fairyland of Arden is invaded by a group of hardhanded "Athenian" workmen who would have been recognizable inhabitants in any Elizabethan village. They are eager to rehearse (well away from prying eyes) a play for performance before the Duke of Athens to celebrate his wedding. As they struggle with their parts in their version of the classical tale of Pyramus and Thisbe, they are revealed as dutiful and well-meaning, but without much experience in acting. Words are muddled and cues are missed.

Shakespeare obviously enjoyed writing their scenes, and although his workmen are amusing, he pays them the compliment of making them real people. Bottom, the weaver, is one of Shakespeare's greatest comic characters, superbly confident in his own ability and master of all situations. Allocated the part of the hero, Pyramus, he is eager to play Thisbe too, and even the lion. Should the lion frighten the ladies, Bottom, as always, has the answer: "I will roar you as gently as any sucking dove," he says. "I will roar you as 'twere any nightingale." The final performance of the play before the duke is a gloriously funny masterpiece in which Shakespeare pokes good-humoured fun at some of the conventions of dramatic writing. Alliteration is now used for comic effect. The moon that has shone on fairies and lovers shines on Pyramus. He is grateful to the moon for shining, "For, by thy gracious, golden, glittering streams, / I trust to taste of truest Thisbe's sight."

"A wood near Athens" becomes even closer to Stratford when a fairy recognizes Oberon's servant Puck as Robin Goodfellow, an impish spirit familiar to all dwellers in the English countryside. Shakespeare must have known this song, popular at the time, called "The Mad Merry Pranks of Robin Goodfellow":

> From Oberon in fairyland the king of ghosts and shadows there
> Mad Robin I, at his command,
> Am sent to view the night sports here:

> What revel rout
> Is kept about
> In every corner where I go
> I will o'er see,
> And merry be
> And make good sport with ho ho ho!

Like the Robin in the song, Shakespeare's Robin enjoys every minute of the "night sports" in the forest. A fairy attendant on Titania has heard all about his "merry pranks" as she asks him:

> Are you not he
> That frights the maidens of the villagery;
> Skim milk, and sometimes labour in the quern
> And bootless make the breathless housewife churn . . . ?

Puck's activities are important in the play, and as he speaks to the audience at the end, he reveals his true identity: "Give me your hands, if we be friends, / And Robin shall restore amends."

It might have been necessary to "restore amends" with some members of his audience. Any die-hard Puritan who had ventured into the playhouse (in order to be able to report on the shocking goings-on, of course) would have sniffed with disapproval. It is surprising that Shakespeare— a child of the Renaissance, educated in the classics, accustomed to attending Protestant services in church every Sunday and hearing fairies, like ghosts, condemned as superstitious "Popish" inventions—should delight in creating a fairy world of such charm and complexity. Nor does he hesitate to introduce other characters from Warwickshire folklore, tales, and ballads—stories condemned as old-fashioned in the light of the new learning. Perhaps Shakespeare *was* just old-fashioned, but he knew his audience, and he more likely realized that pre-Reformation beliefs were still very much alive.

I feel sure he owes his love of fairyland and old tales to stories his mother told him during long winter evenings by the fireside. Mary was an Arden, a member of a minor branch of an illustrious Warwickshire family. Early historians traced their ancestry back to Anglo-Saxon times, and she would have told William that the legendary Saxon hero Guy of Warwick could have been their kinsman. He would have listened to sixteenth-century ballads celebrating Guy's adventures and heard how, after a life of warfare, he returned to Arden to live in the forest as a hermit and rediscover the lady he had loved and lost. (The theme of redemption and reconciliation is central in Shakespeare's romances *Cymbeline*, *The Winter's Tale* and *The Tempest*.) Like most of her generation, Mary had been brought up a Catholic and would have been reluctant to dismiss the medieval past. She would have enjoyed the old tales and taken pleasure in passing this enjoyment on to an eager listener. Perhaps, like Hermione in *The Winter's Tale*, she encouraged young William to tell her stories in return. Hermione asks her son, Mamillius, to "tell's a tale" and he begins promisingly: "There was a man . . . / Dwelt by a churchyard. . . ." Unfortunately, we hear no more. From listening to stories and possibly being encouraged to tell them at an early age, Shakespeare would develop his wonderful "ear" for words—his instinctive feel for their sound and rhythmical effect.

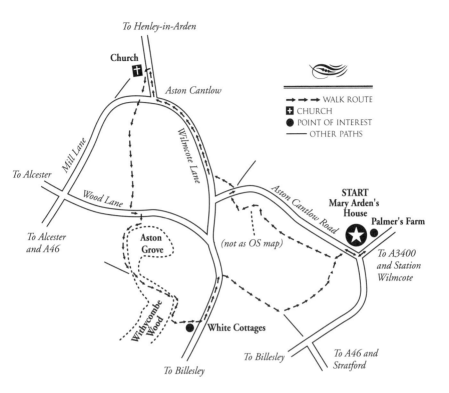

To Henley-in-Arden

Church

Aston Cantlow

Mill Lane

Wilmcote Lane

To Alcester

Wood Lane

To Alcester
and A46

Aston
Grove

(not as OS map)

Aston Cantlow Road

START
Mary Arden's
House

Palmer's Farm

To A3400
and Station
Wilmcote

Withycombe Wood

White Cottages

To Billesley

To Billesley

To Billesley

To A46 and
Stratford

→ → → WALK ROUTE
✚ CHURCH
● POINT OF INTEREST
——— OTHER PATHS

W e begin this walk in the Old World village of
Wilmcote and visit the house where Mary
Arden lived until her marriage. Meadow paths
and quiet lanes lead us to another charming village, Aston
Cantlow, to see the church where she married John
Shakespeare. Our return route winds through one of the
finest of Arden's remaining woodlands, lovely enough to
please the most discerning fairy in A *Midsummer Night's
Dream.*

John would not have had to ride far to visit Mary in
Wilmcote. The village lies in attractive countryside about
three miles northwest of Stratford. Robert Arden's farm,
now known as **Mary Arden's House,** stands in the center
of the village, on the corner of Station Road and the road

to Aston Cantlow. For two hundred years, the striking black-and-white half-timbered house close by, now Palmer's Farm, was thought to be her home, but documentary evidence has now come to light proving that the house on the corner, Glebe Farm, was really her home. The document, dated 1587, mentioned the house being lately in the possession of Agnes Arden, Robert Arden's widow. Both houses are in the care of the Shakespeare Birthplace Trust which, all unknowing, had bought Glebe Farm to prevent the area from being developed for housing!

One can understand the mistake, as the Tudor appearance of Palmer's Farm suggests it was the most likely candidate. The exterior walls of Mary Arden's Tudor home were rebuilt in brick (probably in the eighteenth century), but inside, you will find that a great deal of the original half-timbered house remains. The house was a working farm until the 1960s and many modifications have been made during the centuries, but with the help of one of the Trust's excellent guides, it is possible to see the house as Mary knew it. A long hall with a central fireplace—the smoke escaped through the roof—was the main living room. Mary's father had a chair, and the rest of the family sat on benches around the table—called "the board"—to eat. The main meal generally consisted of stew with flat loaves of bread. Everyone drank ale. A smaller room across the passage from the hall could have been used for sleeping, or for more formal occasions. The dairy led off the hall. According to the guides, with fire being an ever-present risk, it is possible that there was an outside (detached) kitchen. Upstairs, the bedchambers reveal the heavy timbering typical of the early sixteenth century. Mary was the youngest of Robert's eight daughters, and how such a large family contrived to live together in comfort amazes us today! But fortunately, when John Shakespeare came wooing, they might have been able to

Mary Arden's House in Wilmcote

find a little privacy, as by 1557 only Mary and Alice (who appears to have been unmarriageable for some reason) remained with Agnes in the family home. Their father had died the previous year.

Palmer's Farm is the home of the **Shakespeare Countryside Museum.** Many interesting displays bring to life the work and crafts of the countryside around Stratford. The outbuildings include a dovecote and a forge. Children will love the animals. There are Gloucester Old Spot pigs, Cotswold sheep and Longhorn cattle—the most valuable animal on the farm, as it was strong enough to pull a plough and could give milk and meat. There are also exciting falconry displays.

After your visit, leave the house on your right and turn right beside the Aston Cantlow road. Continue along the pavement for about a quarter mile, then turn left along Foxes Lane—you will see a yellow arrow footpath sign. Pass

The half-timbered Guildhall at Aston Cantlow

a gate and some houses, then turn right along a meadow footpath with a fringe of trees concealing houses on your right. Already, you are walking in open rolling countryside, the pleasant Warwickshire meadows that, at the end of *Love's Labour's Lost*, Shakespeare recalls full of flowers in spring:

> When daisies pied and violets blue,
> And lady-smocks all silver-white,
> And cuckoo-buds of yellow hue
> Do paint the meadows with delight....

The path narrows beside a fence on the left. Go through a small gate and keep ahead through another gate to a lane. Here, the path has been diverted for a short distance and differs from the route shown on the Ordnance Survey map, so turn right for about 20 yards, then turn left over a stile. Now you have a splendid wide-ranging view over the valley of the river Alne fringed by low wooded

Walking with William Shakespeare

hills. John Shakespeare must have enjoyed much the same view as he courted Mary, walking with her in country fashion, close to her home. A narrow hedged path leads you downhill, bearing left past a stile, then left again between hedges to a sharp right bend where you rejoin the route marked on the map. Follow the path downhill to go through a gap in the trees to a field. Walk straight across the field to join a track. Bear right along the track to Wilmcote Lane. Turn right along the lane for about 50 yards, then turn left following the yellow arrow footpath sign to go through a gate. Be careful not to take the bridleway on the right (marked with blue arrows). Follow the path ahead beside a field with a hedge on your right. Look left, and soon you will see a post with yellow markings. Cross to the post and keep the same heading, with a hedge now on your left, to rejoin Wilmcote Lane. Turn right and follow the lane as it winds its way for about a mile to the village of **Aston Cantlow.**

This village would have had a special place in the affections of Shakespeare's parents. Wilmcote was in Aston Cantlow parish, and they most likely were married in the **village church.** The entrance to the churchyard is up the little lane opposite the imposing black and white half-timbered Guildhall. Their marriage took place during the reign of the Catholic Queen Mary, who tried to restore Catholicism in England (only to have her efforts defeated after her death by the accession of a Protestant queen, Elizabeth I, in 1558). So John and Mary would have been married with full Catholic rites followed by a Nuptial Mass. As John slipped the ring on Mary's finger, he possibly reflected he had made a wise choice of bride. She was evidently a sensible and responsible girl. She had been trusted by her father to be the executrix of his will, and Robert left her a substantial dowry. Apart from his chief property at Wilmcote, Asbies, and possibly other properties

Aston Cantlow Church, where John Shakespeare likely married Mary Arden

in the area, she inherited a share in the reversion of the Snitterfield estate and the sum of six pounds, thirteen shillings and four pence—quite a large amount of money at that time. It is possible she could read and write, a useful asset for the bride of a businessman. John would have been pleased that he was taking her home to Stratford to the comfortable house in Henley Street he had bought the previous year and that, as his business was thriving, they would be able to afford a few luxuries such as a canopied bed and painted cloths to hang on the walls.

Although the nave of Aston Cantlow Church was remodelled in the nineteenth century, Mary would still feel at home in the thirteenth-century chancel. She would recognize the oak pulpit, carved from local trees sometime in the fifteenth or early sixteenth century, and the octagonal font where she was baptized. The same medieval bells that summon today's worshippers to church would have been rung at her wedding.

Leave the church by the south door and return to the churchyard entrance. Take the signed footpath on your right to follow a path across the churchyard. Go over a stile and follow the narrow path ahead with a hedge on your right, and continue over a wooden bridge to a meadow. There is no clear path at this point, but turn left for a few yards to another wooden bridge on your left. Do not cross the bridge, but turn right to walk over the meadow, keeping a hedge a few yards away on your left. You soon follow a very narrow path that divides. Take the path bearing a little right to cross a stile in the opposite hedge to a lane. Cross to a wide track a few yards to your right on the other side of the lane, and keep ahead with a hedge on your right. When the track curves right, keep straight ahead (with the hedge still on your right) and cross a stile to Wood Lane.

Turn left along Wood Lane for about 100 yards, then leave the lane and take the footpath on the right to walk up the field to the tree-covered slopes of **Aston Grove** and **Withycombe Wood.** These lovely remnants of the great forest of Arden are renowned for their flowers and wildlife and are designated an SSSI—a Site of Special Scientific Interest. The path bears right beside the woods on your left, then goes through a gate to enter the woods and climb through the trees. This is the world in which Shakespeare set *A Midsummer Night's Dream,* so let your imagination run riot among its ancient elms, oaks and beeches! Here you will find the flowers he mentions in his plays, the "pale primrose," "the azur'd harebell," and "daffodils that come before the swallow dares." The trees flourishing in woods like Withycombe must have inspired the imagery used by the fairy queen Titania as, under the influence of the love juice, she lulls Bottom to sleep in her arms:

So doth the woodbine the sweet honeysuckle
Gently entwist; the female ivy so

Enrings the barky fingers of the elm.
O, how I love thee! How I dote on thee!

Follow the path as it rises gradually, then bears left to
leave the wood at the top of the hillside. Turn right to walk
with a fence on your left and the wood on your right. If you
look over the fields on your left, you will see a group of
white cottages. Continue beside the wood until you are
almost level with the cottages, and look carefully for a post
with four footpath signs beside your path. A private path
leads into the wood on your right. Turn left with a hedge
on your right, and walk down the field (leaving the white
cottages on your right) to rejoin Wood Lane. Turn left to
follow the lane for about half a mile. When the road falls
away to the left, turn right to follow the blue bridleway
sign along an attractive grassy path. Shortly, this becomes a
wide track that climbs gently through woods to leave the
trees at a crossing track. Our way follows the blue-arrowed
bridleway almost directly ahead through a metal gate and
into a meadow. If the gate is locked, keep ahead for a few
yards to a stile on the left that grants access to the meadow.
There is no clear path at this point, but bear half-left up
the meadow to the far corner by a hedge. Cross the stile
and turn right (with the hedge on your right) along a good
track that curves left over a sandy gallop. Over the fields
on your right, you will see the rooftops of Wilmcote. Go
through a gate and continue with the hedge still on your
right. The path swings left towards the village to meet our
outbound route. Retrace your steps along Foxes Lane and
turn right to return to Mary Arden's House.

A stream flows through a meadow near Aston Cantlow Church

Starting point
From Stratford, take the A3400 heading north, and after about 3 miles turn left for Wilmcote; or take the A46 heading west and turn right for Wilmcote. GR 164 581.

Parking: In the village.

Public transport
You can travel from Stratford to Wilmcote by train or bus. For times, contact Traveline at (0870) 608 2 608.

Length of walk: 5.5 miles.

Map: Ordnance Survey Explorer Map No. 205.

Refreshments
Two excellent pubs: The Mary Arden Inn and The Mason's Arms. The village shop provides snacks for a picnic.

Mary Arden's House and Palmer's Farm are owned by the Shakespeare Birthplace Trust. All Trust properties are open to the public every day except December 23 to 26. For opening times and admission charges, telephone (01789) 293455 or visit the trust's official website: *www.shakespeare.org.uk*.

L eave Mary Arden's House on your right, and turn right along the Aston Cantlow Road. Turn left along Foxes Lane. After passing houses, turn right and keep ahead to a lane. The footpath has now been diverted and differs from the OS map for a short distance; turn right for a few yards, then turn left over a stile. The path leads downhill bearing left, then left again before turning sharp right to rejoin the route on the map and lead downhill to a field. Cross the field to a track, turn right onto Wilmcote Lane for about 50 yards, then turn left along the footpath to cut the corner and meet Wilmcote Lane again. Turn right along the lane to Aston Cantlow. Turn left up the lane to the church. Take the left footpath (on your right if you visited the church) to cross the churchyard, and follow the path to a meadow. Bear left for a few yards, then right along a narrow path. When the path divides, take the right path to a lane. Cross, and take the track a few yards to your right. When the track curves right, keep straight ahead to Wood Lane. Turn left for about 100 yards, then take the footpath on the right up the field towards Aston Grove and Withycombe Wood. The path bears right along the wood edge, then curves left up through the wood. At the top of the hill, turn right to walk with the wood on your right to a post with several footpath markings. Turn left to walk down the field past white cottages to rejoin Wood Lane. Turn left for about half a mile, then take the path on the right that enters woods and climbs to a crosstrack. Go over the track and through the gate directly ahead into a meadow (or follow the track a little to your right and cross a stile on your left). Bear half-left up the meadow, cross the stile, and turn right to follow the track that swings left to rejoin outbound route in Wilmcote. Retrace your steps along Foxes Lane and turn right to return to Mary Arden's House.

CHAPTER 3

STRATFORD-UPON-AVON AND A WALK TO SHOTTERY

I saw a smith stand with his hammer, thus,
The whilst his iron did on the anvil cool
With open mouth swallowed a tailor's news
Who, with his shears and measure in his hand,
Standing on slippers, which his nimble haste
Had falsely thrust upon contrary feet,
Told of many a thousand warlike French

. . . .

Another lean and unwashed artificer
Cuts off his tale. . . .
—Hubert De Burgh, *King John*

In just a few words, Shakespeare describes a scene familiar to us all: a group of people sharing exciting news. With his keen eye, he brings each one vividly alive as they react in their different, very human ways. With a chuckle, he notes that the tailor, in his rush to tell his story, has his slippers on the wrong feet! This ability to portray real, recognizable people is one of Shakespeare's greatest strengths. From his earliest days, as he stood in the doorway of his father's workshop in Henley Street, the thriving market town of Stratford helped to provide the inspiration he needed.

William was born in Stratford on or around April 23, 1564. He was John and Mary Shakespeare's third child and eldest son. Two daughters had died in infancy. The exact date of his birth is not recorded, but the date of his christening in Stratford's Holy Trinity Church, April 25, is entered in the church register. At that time, infant mortality was very high—a third of all children died before they reached adulthood—so his father would have lost no time in arranging William's christening. The deaths of two daughters already would have made his parents even more anxious. To make matters worse, when William was two months old, a devastating outbreak of bubonic plague reached Stratford. The number of victims increased daily, particularly among the elderly and the very young. As Mary held her precious baby son in her arms, she would have heard the passing bell for the dead ringing almost unceasingly from Holy Trinity Church down by the river. So how did William survive? It could have been good luck, of course, but I believe it is likely that Mary took him away from the insanitary town, over the fields to the healthier air of Wilmcote. She could have stayed in her old home— her mother, Agnes, lived in the house until her death in 1580—but if her mother felt it would be unwise to shelter a refugee from Stratford, Mary could have stayed on her own property, Asbies, where she owned a cottage. Recent investigations into the Arden estates have revealed that her cottage still stands across a paddock from her old home. Now called Pear Tree Cottage, it is a delightful place to stay, offering bed and breakfast accommodation. You could sleep under the same roof that possibly sheltered Mary and baby William! It is significant that out of a population of around two thousand in Stratford, two hundred people died of the plague, but in Wilmcote there were no deaths. After the heat of the summer had passed and the cooler months lessened the effects of the plague, Mary could have returned safely to Henley Street.

After William, the Shakespeares had five more children. Gilbert was born in 1566 and Joan in 1569. Anne, born in 1571, died at the age of eight. Richard, born in 1574, appears to have lived in Stratford all his life and died unmarried at age thirty-nine. William's youngest brother, Edmund, born in 1580, also became an actor but died in London when he was twenty-seven. Mary would have had her hands full caring for her large family, but she may have found time to help her husband in his workshop, which occupied one end of the house. At busy times, the older children (especially William, as the eldest son) would have been called upon to help. John made and sold gloves, but he also dealt in local goods: wool from the Cotswolds, barley from the Feldon, and timber from the Forest of Arden. He was also a "whitawer"—a craftsman who worked with delicate white skins. William knew all about leatherworking and refers to the trade several times in his plays. He knew the quality of each skin. One of the most delicate was "cheveril," the skin of a young goat. This stretched easily, and in *Romeo and Juliet*, the daredevil Mercutio uses an image from the leatherworker's trade to criticise Romeo for a weak joke: "O, here's a wit of cheveril, that stretches from an inch narrow to an ell broad."

A counter opened from John Shakespeare's workshop to the street, where passers-by could purchase gloves and other leather items such as drawstring purses and—if they had the status of gentlemen—holders for their swords. Although in William's day Stratford was a small town, it bustled with life, and Henley Street was one of the main thoroughfares, lined with a wide range of shops and small businesses. Apart from Shakespeare's father, there were other glovemakers in Henley Street. Trade would have been brisk, as gloves were an important item in the wardrobe of the well-dressed Elizabethan. They were often richly decorated on the back and cuffs, and given as presents. In *Much Ado About Nothing*, Count Claudio sends a pair to Hero, whom he intends to marry.

Stratford was particularly busy on market days, which were held every Thursday, when people from the surrounding villages flocked into the town to exchange their farm produce for manufactured goods. With its splendid bridge spanning the Avon, linking the cattle farms of the Forest of Arden north of the town with the open fields of the Feldon south of the river, Stratford made an ideal center for the exchange of their different types of produce. Barley grew well in the rich soil of the Feldon, and Stratford was famous for its malting. The quality of the local beer was ensured by the appointment of an official ale-taster, a position held by William's father in 1557.

On September 14, Holy Rood Day, a trade fair was held. Stratford must have been noisier and more lively than ever. Among the crowds, workers were hired and paid, freelance dealers bought up country goods to be sold at a profit in the larger towns, and pedlars like Autolycus in *The Winter's Tale* tempted the country folk with their laces and ballads. London was a hundred miles away, but Greenways, the Stratford carriers, made the journey to the great metropolis every fortnight, taking the small town's

Stratford Grammar School (now the King Edward VI Grammar School). The beautifully timbered roof of "Big School," the room where it is believed Shakespeare was educated.

produce for sale and returning with orders and luxuries like the sugar and dates enjoyed at the sheep shearing feast in *The Winter's Tale*. Letters could also be carried. In November, 1581, they took a letter, two cheeses, a loaf, and five shillings to Robert Debdale, a relative of William's mother. Debdale was a Jesuit priest, a member of the Catholic order endeavouring to support and possibly restore the old religion in England. He had been imprisoned in the Tower and tortured but was allowed contact with his family.

And Stratford had more to offer William as he grew up. In the thirteenth century, a religious foundation, the Guild of the Holy Cross, had built a chapel in Church Street, founded a school attached to the Guild buildings (where William was to receive an excellent education),

Walking with William Shakespeare

and erected a row of almshouses for the poor of the town. These had been rebuilt around 1490 by Sir Hugh Clopton, who had left Stratford to grow rich in London. He also built the bridge across the Avon, and New Place (the "pretty house of brick and timber" that Shakespeare bought in 1597, having followed Sir Hugh's example!). With the coming of the Reformation, church property passed into lay hands, and the Guild was dissolved in 1547. In 1553, Stratford was granted a charter of incorporation. The town's affairs became the concern of a council comprising fourteen aldermen and fourteen burgesses. The council was headed by the mayor, known as the high bailiff (a title adopted to satisfy the local lord of the manor, whose attempts to interfere with the town's affairs were stoutly resisted by the fledgling council.) The Guild property and its responsibilities for the school and the poor passed into the council's hands.

The principal tradesmen of the town soon became the council's most prominent members. These included William's father, who was elected an alderman in 1565. He was now entitled to wear a black furred gown and a special ring recalled by his son in *Romeo and Juliet*: Strange dreams, Mercutio informs Romeo, are due to the influence of Queen Mab, the fairies' midwife, who "comes in shape no bigger than an agate-stone on the fore-finger of an alderman." John was responsible for overseeing the town's accounts, which he signed with the mark of his trade—a pair of glover's compasses. (This did not necessarily mean he could not write, as friends known to be literate also signed with their marks.) He reached the height of his public career in 1569 when he was elected high bailiff and a justice of the peace. He was president of the Court of Record (assessor of small fines), clerk of the market, coroner, and almoner. He also had to supervise the fairs and those responsible for bridges and highways, the chapel, and the parish church. Until the end of 1576, he attended every council meeting. But after the end of that year he attended on just one occasion, to support the election of a close friend.

John's business declined. He began to mortgage his property and Mary's to pay his debts and in 1591 pleaded that he dare not go to church (attendance was compulsory) for fear of being arrested for debt. Was John merely suffering from the general slowdown in the rural economy that affected the nation towards the close of the sixteenth century, and risking his money carelessly by standing surety for debtors who were unable to pay? Or was his plea just an excuse to avoid church because he felt he could no longer take Protestant communion? In 1751, a handwritten Catholic *Testament of the Soul* was discovered concealed between the rafters of his Henley Street house. Had John received the *Testament*, a late Tudor-era document, from the Jesuit Edmund Campion, sent from Rome to support and encourage Catholicism in England? Each page was signed in John Shakespeare's name and asked for prayers and masses to be said for his soul after his death—a request that went against Protestant teaching. Was John reverting to Catholicism, the religion of his youth? Heavy fines were imposed on known Catholics who refused to conform. The houses of people believed to be Catholics were often searched, and John, fearing for his safety, may have hastily hidden the incriminating document. Unfortunately, the *Testament* has been lost.

Whatever the reason for John's plea, the result, as we shall see later, had an important effect on the lives of his family—particularly on that of his eldest son, William.

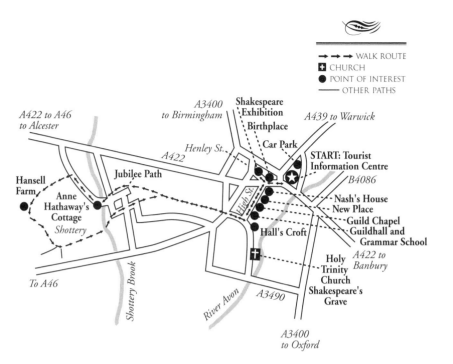

A3400
to Birmingham

Shakespeare
Exhibition
Birthplace

A439 to Warwick

A422 to A46
to Alcester

Henley St.
A422

Car Park

START: Tourist
Information Centre

B4086

Hansell
Farm

Jubilee Path

Anne
Hathaway's
Cottage

Shottery

High St.

Nash's House
New Place
Guild Chapel
Guildhall and
Grammar School

Hall's Croft

A422 to
Banbury

To A46

Shottery Brook

River Avon

A3490

Holy
Trinity
Church
Shakespeare's
Grave

A3400
to Oxford

T his walk begins with a visit to John Shakespeare's
house in Henley Street (now known as the
Birthplace in honor of his famous son) and
continues on to some of the other fascinating places in
Stratford intimately connected with the great playwright.
Our starting point is the Tourist Information Centre at the
foot of Bridge Street. Across the road in **Bancroft Gardens**
stands the **Shakespeare Monument** presented to the town
by Lord Gower in 1888. The poet sits looking thoughtful,
surrounded by life-size statues of some of his best known
characters: Prince Hal of Agincourt fame, Hamlet
contemplating the skull of Yorick, Falstaff the fat knight,
and Lady Macbeth vainly trying to wash Duncan's blood
off her hands. In Shakespeare's time, cattle grazed on
Bancroft and the young men of the town practiced archery.
William would have been among them. In *The Merchant of*

Venice, Bassanio uses an image from archery to ask his friend Antonio to lend him more money:

> In my school-days, when I had lost one shaft,
> I shot his fellow of the selfsame flight
> The selfsame way with more advised watch,
> To find the other forth; and by advent'ring both,
> I oft found both.

From the Tourist Information Centre, turn right to walk up Bridge Street past Barclays Bank, which stands on the site of the former Market Cross. Continue up Bridge Street to a roundabout. Bear left past the junction with Union Street to walk up Henley Street. Young William must have run up and down this street many times! You will see the black-and-white half-timbered house where he was most likely born—now known as **Shakespeare's Birthplace**—on the right side of the road. If you stand facing the house, the left side of the building was the family home; on the right was John's workshop.

Begin your tour of the Birthplace with a stop in the excellent visitor center. A fascinating exhibition takes you into Shakespeare's world and tells the story of his life. The exhibition includes many original items, including a desk in use when William learned his lessons in the great timber-framed schoolroom of Stratford's fifteenth-century grammar school, and a first edition of his plays. There is a detailed scale model of the theater where so many of his greatest plays were acted—the Globe on Bankside in London—and the poet can be seen sitting, quill pen at the ready, in a reconstruction of his study.

Upon entering the Birthplace, the first room you see is the parlor—the family living room—carefully furnished based on evidence provided by other craftsmen's houses of the time. It is rather surprising to see a canopied and

The Shakespeare Monument in Bancroft Gardens, presented to Stratford by Lord Gower

draped four-poster bed occupying part of the room! Evidently, this would be the family's best bed, always reserved for guests. Travel, particularly at night, was difficult and dangerous, and here Mary could provide a comfortable night's rest for perhaps a merchant visiting John, or a friend from the country who had been selling produce in the market.

The family ate at a long table in the hall, which has its large original fireplace, complete with a spit for roasting. The table is set with pewter plates, a luxury John would have been able to afford before he ran into debt. At the far end of the house, John's workshop has been reconstructed with examples of the leathers and tools he used. Upstairs, one of the bedchambers, according to tradition, is the actual room where Shakespeare was born. The room, with its four-poster bed hung with red and green drapes, feels homely and comfortable. Beneath the main bed is a wheeled truckle bed which could be used for children. The toys, baby clothes and cradle are authentic replicas of sixteenth-century originals.

What was home life like for William growing up in Henley Street? There is no direct evidence, but I feel he had a happy childhood. His family must have enjoyed his sense of fun, so evident in his plays, and his pleasing personality, which was noted by all his contemporaries. In spite of financial problems, his father is remembered by Sir John Mennes, who saw him in his shop, as "a merry-cheekt old man who said 'Will was a good honest fellow, but he dared have crackt a jest with him at any time.' " Perhaps in *Measure for Measure*, Shakespeare was recalling his own childhood when he wrote about kindly parents who

> Having bound up the threatening twigs of birch
> Only to stick it in their children's sight
> For terror, not to use, in time the rod
> Becomes more mocked than feared. . . .

There is a great deal more to see, and the Birthplace Trust's enthusiastic and knowledgeable guides make sure you enjoy your visit. The garden is beautifully maintained and planted with many of the flowers and herbs mentioned by Shakespeare. The bed of old-fashioned roses would have delighted him. They were his favorite flower.

To continue our walk, leave the Birthplace on your left and retrace your steps down Henley Street to the roundabout. Cross the top of Wood Street and bear right down the High Street. Adjoining the Garrick Inn on the right is the richly carved exterior of **Harvard House,** dated 1596. It was built by Thomas Rogers, a prosperous merchant. His daughter Katherine married a London man, Robert Harvard, and it was their son John who founded the famous American university. The house is now a museum with a fine collection of pewter artifacts spanning two thousand years of history.

Cross the junction with Ely Street and Sheep Street. (High Street now becomes Chapel Street.) Walk down Chapel Street to the corner of Chapel Lane, where **Nash's**

House, a striking half-timbered building, adjoins the site of **New Place,** the house bought by Shakespeare for his retirement. Nash's House, also owned by the Birthplace Trust, belonged to Thomas Nash, who married Elizabeth Hall, Shakespeare's granddaughter. Elizabeth was the only child of Shakespeare's elder daughter, Susanna. Nash's House is furnished in the style of the early seventeenth century. Don't miss the charming portrait of Elizabeth and Thomas. The upstairs rooms house Stratford's local history museum.

Only the foundations of New Place remain, now in an attractive garden setting. The house was demolished in 1759 by the Reverend Gastrell to spite the Stratford Town Council, which (unfairly, in his opinion) had insisted he should pay his taxes. He claimed he owed no money because he spent only part of his time in the town. He also chopped down a mulberry tree said to have been planted by Shakespeare. Soon, pieces of the tree were turned into "tobacco-stoppers" to be sold in Birmingham market! The beautiful grounds include an Elizabethan knot garden, patterned with low trimmed hedges enclosing beds of flowers grown in Shakespeare's time, and the Great Garden, an ideal place to relax. A cutting from the mulberry tree has pride of place on the lawn.

The **Guild Chapel,** still used by pupils of the Stratford Grammar School (now called the King Edward VI Grammar School) that Shakespeare once attended, stands on the opposite corner of Chapel Lane. In 1563, John Shakespeare (as town chamberlain) was ordered by the Protestant authorities to cover the medieval wall paintings with limewash. Traces of the splendid mural of the last judgment, known as "Doom," can still be seen above the chancel arch. The half-timbered **Guildhall** is next door. Today, the upper floor is still a schoolroom kept as it was when young William Shakespeare sat at one of the desks.

The Birthplace in Henley Street. It is most likely Shakespeare was born in this house.

Although no sixteenth-century academic records survive for Stratford's grammar school, the sons of the town's burgesses were educated free, and John would surely have taken advantage of a grammar school education for his son. Before entering "Big School," as the schoolroom was called (and still is), at the age of seven, William would have learned his letters from his hornbook—a piece of paper, bearing the alphabet and the Lord's Prayer, held between a sheet of transparent horn and a wooden frame with a handle. (The first row of the alphabet began with a cross. In *Richard III*, King Edward, suspicious of his brother George, Duke of Clarence, "from the cross-row plucks the letter G.")

So, probably around 1571, William began his grammar school education. Instruction was based on Latin, the key to the professions: law, medicine and the church. In the lower school, the boys learned their Latin grammar by heart from William Lily's textbook *Short Introduction of Grammar*, prescribed for use in all schools. In *The Merry Wives of Windsor*, Sir Hugh Evans tests the Latin of young William Page, recalling the opening page of Lily's book, which explains nouns. While still in the lower school, William read some classical drama, mostly comedies that provided the inspiration for early plays such as *The Two Gentlemen of Verona*. After three years, he moved into the upper school to speak Latin at all times and be taught to think and speak logically and convincingly.

Among other classical writers to whom he was introduced, the great Roman poet Ovid held Shakespeare spellbound with his tales of the gods and goddesses of the ancient world. There are many references to Ovid throughout Shakespeare's plays. His favourite book was Ovid's *Metamorphoses* ("the book of changes") in which the poet tells how the gods assume different forms and nothing remains constant. When Shakespeare wrote his first long poem to try to win a patron, he chose a story from Ovid. Shakespeare's *Venus and Adonis*, prefaced by a quotation from Ovid, was an overnight success. One of his contemporaries, Francis Meres, recognized that Shakespeare's verse was inspired by Ovid. "The sweet witty soul of Ovid," he wrote, "lives in mellifluous and honey-tongued Shakespeare."

Elizabethan education placed great emphasis on training the memory. Books were scarce and the authors read at school had to stand one in good stead throughout life. Could there have been a better training for a budding actor?

It was vitally important in Elizabeth's England that the rising generation should attend church regularly and be well-grounded in the Protestant faith. Apart from the readings from the Bible, the Psalms and the Prayer Book that William would have heard in church, every schoolday

Stratford Grammar School (now the King Edward VI Grammar School) with the Guild Chapel in the background

began and ended with a service. From his earliest years, his retentive memory was enriched by the beautiful phrasing of the English translations of the Bible, particularly the Bishops' revision of 1568, with its balanced rhythms and homely imagery. One hears echoes of the Bible and the Prayer Book in all his plays.

Did William enjoy his schooldays? It is hard to imagine that even the most dedicated student would not have yawned through some of the lessons! William had to be sitting at his desk looking respectable by six o'clock in the morning in summer and by seven in winter. There would be a short break for breakfast around nine, then lessons until around eleven-thirty. He had two hours for dinner, which he took at home. There would not be much time to eat, as he would be expected to help lay the table and wait on his parents before he had his own meal. Afternoon lessons began at one-thirty and continued until five-thirty, with a short break midafternoon. Wednesdays

Walking with William Shakespeare

and Saturdays were half-holidays, and there were around forty non-schooldays each year. Discipline was severe. No wonder that in *As You Like It* we hear about

> the whining schoolboy, with his satchel
> And shining morning face, creeping like a snail
> Unwillingly to school. . . .

But life in Stratford could be exciting for William, particularly when the players came to town. The first company of actors, the Queen's Players, came during the year his father was bailiff in August 1569. Five-year-old William may have sat with his father and the rest of the council in the Guildhall to approve the actors' performance before they were allowed to put on their plays in the inn-yards on Bridge Street. From that time, various companies visited Stratford and were well-received. The townspeople also performed their own amateur theatricals, and in *The Two Gentlemen of Verona* Shakespeare recalls one in which he may have taken part. One of the heroines, Julia, describes her role in Whitsun festivities:

> at Pentecost,
> When all our pageants of delight were play'd
> Our youth got me to play the woman's part.

By the time William was approaching fourteen or fifteen, as we have seen, his father's fortunes had altered dramatically. He was deeply in debt and no longer held any public office. Gone were the furred robe and the alderman's ring. Normally, a young man with a good grammar school education could consider going to a university or entering one of the Inns of Court to be trained as a lawyer. But it seems that neither avenue was open to William. On account of his father's troubles, it is likely that he left school early, possibly before he was sixteen. Perhaps he helped his father in the shop or worked in a lawyer's office. His plays reveal a wide knowledge of legal terms, but he could have become familiar with these among his Stratford neighbors, who were constantly suing each other (usually for debt). Whatever his occupation, his interests lay elsewhere. He was young and in love, and around the age of eighteen we find him setting off for Hewland's Farm in **Shottery,** a small village a mile or so west of Stratford, to woo a young woman called Anne Hathaway.

We follow William to Shottery along a route such as the one Celia describes in *As You Like It*: "west of this place, down in the neighbour bottom." So continue down Church Street (formerly Chapel Street before you crossed the intersection). Pass the school and almshouses on your left, and take the next road on the right, Chestnut Walk, to a road junction. Cross two roads, and follow the entry immediately ahead signed on the left wall for Anne Hathaway's Cottage. Keep ahead, following the signs for the cottage between walls and fences, and crossing several roads. Over a bridge, a tree-shaded path leads you to a large recreation ground. Shakespeare probably came this way, but most of his route would have been over open country, and the recreation ground would have been farmers' fields. Follow the path over the recreation ground, and when the way divides, take the right hand path signed "Anne Hathaway's Cottage via Tavern Lane." Pass some attractive cottages and a garden center to a road island near the Bell Inn in Shottery.

You can keep straight ahead along Cottage Lane to Anne Hathaway's Cottage, but usually you can arrive at the cottage by a route that runs parallel with the lane, along the lovely wooded **Jubilee Path.** You will see the steps leading to the entrance to the Jubilee Path across the road a little to your right. The path dips downhill, then

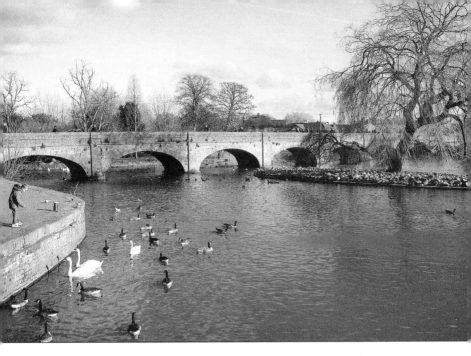

Feeding the swans on the river Avon, with medieval Clopton Bridge in the background

turns left to cross the bridge over the Shottery Brook. More of Celia's directions seem to apply at this point, as she says:

> The rank of osiers, by the murmuring stream,
> Left on your right hand, brings you to the place.

The Jubilee Path leaves the willow-bordered stream on your left, of course, but Shakespeare would presumably have been following Cottage Lane on the other side of the stream. The path was created to celebrate the Silver Jubilee of the second Queen Elizabeth!

Across the road, in its beautiful garden setting, is **Anne Hathaway's Cottage.** This must be everyone's idea of a typically English, Old World home—heavily timbered, with a thatched roof and small windows with diamond-leaded panes. The house is built on a slope. If you stand in the garden facing the cottage, the lower portion, which dates from the fifteenth century, was the extent of the house in which Anne Hathaway grew up. The rest was added in the seventeenth century, possibly by Anne's eldest brother, Bartholomew. Inside, the hall, with its great open fireplace, was the family's main living room. It is said that William courted Anne on the winged elm-boarded settle beside the fire but, sadly, we were told it probably dates from a later period. In any case, given its narrow seat and upright back, I feel sure they would soon have found somewhere more comfortable! The kitchen is dominated by another open fireplace with a bread oven to the left of the hearth. It retains its elm "stop" or door. Many interesting furnishings include a large lidded chest for storing flour called a "bread ark." The lid would fold back to provide a firm base for kneading the dough. Upstairs, the roof is supported by curved timbers in the shape of an inverted V. This building method, known as "cruck construction," was popular in the fifteenth century. In an upstairs room you will find what must have been one of the family's treasures: a finely carved oak four-poster bed.

Outside, there is a lovely view of the house from the orchard and the **Shakespeare Tree Garden,** planted in 1988 with trees mentioned in his plays.

To see some of the countryside where William walked with Anne, leave the cottage on your left and continue up Cottage Lane. Just after passing the picturesque cottages of Shottery Hamlet on your right, turn left and follow the footpath sign up the tarmac drive to Hansell Farm. Just in front of the farm buildings, turn left to cross a stile, and keep ahead between fences to go through a gate. You are now on the crest of a hill; look east for a splendid view of Stratford. On the skyline you will see the **Welcombe Monument,** which we visit in chapter 10.

From the gate, bear left, then keep to the path as it swings right to enter woods. After about fifty yards you come to a crosspath. Turn left. (Our path is edged with low wood supports.) The path runs between hedges, then past a pinewood and houses to become a wide track meeting a road by Shottery St. Andrew's National School. Turn left to a road junction. Go right here, and follow the road as it bends right past more attractive thatched cottages. Just round the corner, take the footpath on the left, which leads you back in the direction of the recreation ground. At the entrance, bear right to retrace your steps over the recreation ground to return to Stratford.

The streamside approach to Anne Hathaway's cottage in Shottery

Starting Point:
Stratford Tourist Information Centre. GR 204 550.

Parking: Avonside car park.

Length of walk: 4 miles.

Map: Ordnance Survey Explorer Map No. 205.

The Shakespeare Houses include the Birthplace, Anne Hathaway's Cottage, Nash's House, and the gardens of New Place. The Shakespeare Houses also include Hall's Croft (which we visit in chapter 11), and Mary Arden's House, Palmer's Farm, and the Shakespeare Countryside Museum (see chapter 2). All the houses are maintained by the Shakespeare Birthplace Trust, which provides excellent guides. The houses are open every day year-round except December 23 to 26. For details of opening times and admission charges, telephone (01789) 204016 or visit the official website: *www.shakespeare.org.uk.*

From the Tourist Information Centre, turn right and walk up Bridge Street. Bear left at the roundabout past the junction with Union Street to walk up Henley Street and reach the Shakespeare Exhibition and Shakespeare's Birthplace. Retrace the route down Henley Street, cross the top of Wood Street, and bear right down High Street. Harvard House and Garrick Inn sit on the right. Continue down Chapel Street to Nash's House and New Place gardens, on the left at the corner of Chapel Lane. See the Guild Chapel, Guildhall, grammar school and almshouses. Turn right along Chestnut Walk to the road junction. Cross two roads, and take the footpath ahead through the entry signed on left wall for Anne Hathaway's Cottage. Continue ahead, crossing several roads, then follow the path over the recreation ground. At the division, take the right-hand path signed "Anne Hathaway's Cottage via Tavern Lane" to a road in Shottery near the Bell Inn. Follow Cottage Lane to the cottage, or take the Jubilee Path over the road a little to your right to cross the Shottery Brook. Leave the cottage on your left, and continue along Cottage Lane. Turn left for Hansell Farm. Just before the farm buildings, turn left over a stile and continue to go through a gate. Bear left, and keep to the path as it swings right (through woods) to a crosspath. Turn left to a road by a school. Turn left to a road junction. Turn right to a sharp right bend. Just past the corner, take the footpath on your left to return to the recreation ground. At the entrance, bear right to retrace your steps to Stratford.

CHAPTER 4

SHAKESPEARE'S TWO ANNES:
MARRIAGE AND TEMPLE GRAFTON

O spirit of love, how quick and fresh art thou!
—Orsino, Duke of Illyria, *Twelfth Night*

Around harvest time, 1582, Shakespeare and Anne Hathaway must have anticipated marriage, for by the end of November, Anne was three months pregnant. Shakespeare was eighteen; Anne, twenty-six. Perhaps they felt that a simple vow to marry, holding hands in front of their relatives and promising to forsake all other friends, was sufficient. Such betrothal ceremonies were recognized at that time as a form of marriage allowing couples to sleep together, and were accepted by long tradition by many in the community. But they carried with them no legal guarantee that after the death of one of the betrothed couple, the surviving spouse or children would have any rights to inherit the deceased's property. The civil courts recognized only church weddings. Anne came from a respectable family with whom Shakespeare's father had done business. They would have to marry and there was no time to lose: no marriages could be solemnized during Advent, which was fast approaching, and after Christmas Anne's pregnancy would be increasingly obvious.

Now we are confronted with a puzzle from which we can deduce some fascinating theories but no real answers. Stratford was in the diocese of Worcester, and Shakespeare, presumably alone and in haste, rode to Worcester to get a marriage license. He was successful. But the entry in the Episcopal Register for November 27 records the granting of a marriage license to one William Shakespeare and a lady called Anne Whateley of Temple Grafton! How was it that no one noticed the mistake? Or was it really an error? Who is this mysterious lady, residing in a small village five miles from Stratford?

There was time before Advent for only one calling of the banns—perhaps at the church door before the wedding. So in order to indemnify the Church authorities from any legal problems that might arise after such short notice, the next day, November 28, two farming friends of the

Hathaway family, Fulk Sandells and John Richardson, rode from Shottery to Worcester and agreed to a bond of forty pounds (a large sum of money in those days). The record of the bond in the Episcopal Register states, as we might expect, that "William Shakespeare and Anne Hathaway of Stratford in the diocese of Worcester, maiden, may lawfully solemnize matrimony together and in the same afterwards remain and continue like man and wife."

How did this confusion come about? I suspect the entry for the bond must be correct, as money is involved, but how did the clerk muddle the entries? It could be a genuine mistake. The clerk had been involved in a case with a family of Whateleys earlier in the day. Two "Annes" might have misled him, but how could he confuse Temple Grafton with Stratford?

Did Shakespeare intend to marry the other Anne? A handsome young man, blessed (as Nicholas Rowe, an early biographer, records in his *Life of Mr. William Shakespear*) with wit and "great sweetness in his manners," must have broken a few hearts around Stratford. Beauty in all its aspects would not be lost on a budding poet who was to sing so merrily about "a lover and his lass" and depict the ecstasy and agony of young love with such intensity in *Romeo and Juliet*. Did he find an attractive woman's charms impossible to resist? As Berowne says in one of Shakespeare's earliest plays, *Love's Labour's Lost*, "where is any author in the world, teaches such beauty as a woman's eye?"

Another consideration strengthens Anne Whateley's claim to exist. According to the entry on the license, she lived in Temple Grafton, so presumably the marriage would be celebrated in the village church. A family of Whateleys, drapers by trade, were neighbours of the Shakespeares in Henley Street. They were a highly respectable family but remained staunch Catholics willing to pay fines for non-

Temple Grafton Church, where I believe Shakespeare could have married Anne Hathaway

attendance at Protestant services. The Stratford vicar at that time was Henry Haycroft, an ardent Protestant. If Anne Whateley was related to the Stratford family and shared the same faith, she could have preferred to be married at Temple Grafton where the vicar, John Frith, was an old priest still happy to break the law and perform Catholic ceremonies. It is just possible that Shakespeare intended to marry Anne Whateley and had made arrangements for the wedding at Temple Grafton beforehand!

But whether there was another Anne in his life or not, William Shakespeare married Anne Hathaway, probably on November 30. (Incidentally he did not marry her for her money. Her father, who had died in 1581, left her only a small dowry and no land or property.) But where?

According to the law they should have been married in their own parish church in Stratford, but there is no record of their marriage in the church register. (Although the register bears the date 1600, this was the year in which the entries from 1558 were entered from existing records, authenticated by the signatures of the vicar and the churchwardens.) A dispensation could be granted on "grounds of reasonable secrecy," but there seems little point, as both families shared the same social standing and Anne's pregnancy would not have been obvious.

No record of Shakespeare's marriage exists in any church. Can we presume that the clerk who recorded the wording of his marriage license mistakenly wrote Anne Whateley instead of Anne Hathaway, but that he was correct in stating that Temple Grafton was the church Shakespeare and Anne Hathaway had chosen for their wedding? The jury is still out on these questions! But I am inclined to believe that was the case. The clerk could have confused the two Annes—he had had a busy morning and perhaps enjoyed a convivial dinner—but he made no mistake when he recorded Temple Grafton as the church where the wedding was to take place. Anne could have been living in Temple Grafton for a short time after her father's death or could have stayed there for the required fifteen days to qualify for marriage in the village church. But why should they choose a small village, in the heart of the countryside, at an awkward distance for family and friends to travel, particularly in November when the roads would probably have been more treacherous than ever?

To find a possible answer, we must return to John Frith, Temple Grafton's accommodating vicar. England was now officially a Protestant state, but many of Queen Elizabeth's subjects, like the Whateleys, clung to the old faith. Perhaps Shakespeare and Anne and their parents wanted a Catholic wedding celebrated with Nuptial Mass.

Walking with William Shakespeare

It is likely that Shakespeare's mother, an Arden and a member of a strongly Catholic family, would have wanted a Catholic wedding for her son. He was still a minor, answerable to his parent's wishes. Anne's father was dead, leaving her with a stepmother who may have taken little interest in her affairs. John Frith, the old vicar at Temple Grafton, would grant their request. Naturally, the Protestant authorities disapproved of him, commenting sourly that he was "an old priest unsound of religion . . . he can neither preach nor read well; his chiefest trade is to cure hawks that are hurt and diseased, for which purpose many do usually repair to him."

Surprisingly for the times, Shakespeare, unlike the authorities, would approve of the old priest. In a violent age, he shared the priest's concern when faced with suffering in all its forms. In *Venus and Adonis*, he feels for the hunted hare, desperately trying to evade the hounds as they close in on him:

> Then shalt thou see the dew-bedabbled wretch,
> Turn and return, indenting with the way;
> Each envious briar his weary legs doth scratch.

Even the most unregarded of creatures wins his sympathy. He notes in the same poem

> the snail, whose tender horns being hit,
> Shrinks backward in his shelly cave with pain.

Again surprisingly, over forty years after Henry VIII ordered the destruction of the monasteries, we find Shakespeare, in spite of his Protestant education, painting portraits of kindly friars—members of monastic orders. Perhaps he recalled John Frith when he created the character of Friar Lawrence in *Romeo and Juliet*. We first meet the friar filling his basket with "precious-juiced flowers." As he selects plants that can heal, he reflects on how if they are misused, even by accident, they can also destroy—a sad foreshadowing of the failure of his well-meant plan to reunite the lovers and their warring families. Although his plan does fail and contributes to the tragic situation at the end of the play, his motives are judged to be blameless. Having heard Friar Lawrence's honest account of his part in the tragedy, the Prince of Verona comments, "We still have known thee for a holy man."

In *Much Ado About Nothing*, Friar Francis comes to the rescue after Hero is slandered on her wedding day and spurned by Claudio, the man she is about to marry. Convinced of Hero's innocence, the friar suggests Claudio should be led to believe she died of grief. His plan is successful, winning time for Hero's innocence to be proved and Claudio to feel remorse. It is owing to the wisdom of Friar Francis that the play concludes happily. However "unsound of religion" these old priests may have been, Shakespeare remembers them with affection.

So I believe Shakespeare, as well as his parents, could have asked John Frith to officiate at his wedding and that the ceremony took place in the little village church at Temple Grafton at the end of November 1582—a November wedding for a poet who so loved the spring, celebrated in one of his songs as "the only pretty ring time"!

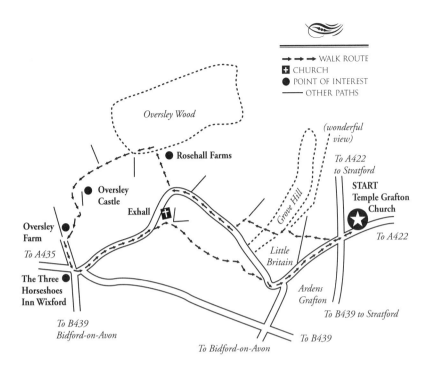

WALK ROUTE
CHURCH
POINT OF INTEREST
OTHER PATHS

Oversley Wood

(wonderful view)

● Rosehall Farms

To A422
to Stratford

START
Temple Grafton
Church

● Oversley Castle

Exhall

Grove Hill

To A422

Oversley Farm

To A435

Little Britain

The Three Horseshoes Inn Wixford ●

Ardens Grafton

To B439 to Stratford

To B439
Bidford-on-Avon

To B439

To Bidford-on-Avon

T his walk starts from **Temple Grafton Church** and follows footpaths and lanes to Exhall, Wixford and Arden's Grafton through beautiful countryside which Shakespeare knew well. Perhaps too well! Francis Wise, Radcliffe Librarian at Oxford in the mid-eighteenth century, was possibly the anonymous author of a "Letter from the place of Shakespeare's Nativity" published in the *British Magazine* in 1762. The letter claimed that young Shakespeare "loved a glass for the pleasure of society," and that when he and his friends represented Stratford in a drinking competition with the "Bidford Sippers," he ended up spending the night by the roadside under a crab apple tree! In the morning he was urged to resume the contest but declined, offering his friends his thoughts on

Our path through Oversley Wood, bordered with bluebells in May

neighboring villages instead. Among them he listed "Hungry Grafton, Dudgeing [dodging?] Exhall, Papist Wixford and Drunken Bidford."

Leave the church on your right and walk up the road. Keep ahead over the crossroads. After a few yards, take the footpath on your right, following a wide path over open countryside. Go over a crosspath and continue to cross a stile. Now you are standing on the top of **Grove Hill.** The wooded hillside drops away at your feet to reveal a magnificent view over the **Avon Valley.** On a clear day, it is possible to see the Malvern Hills. Some of Shakespeare's favorite wildflowers—cowslips, primroses, and violets—carpet the hillside in spring.

Turn left along the brow of the hill for about 100 yards, then turn right down some steps to descend the steep hillside. Go through a gate and bear half-left (still downhill) to a waymarked post. Cross the stile at the foot of the hill and continue over a field to a farm track where you turn left to a lane. Turn right and follow the quiet lane towards Exhall for about three-quarters of a mile. Pass the tall gates of Valley Farm and after a few yards turn right along the asphalt approach to Rosehall Farm, signed as a bridleway. Pass the farm, go through a gate, and follow a grassy path ahead to go through another gate at the edge of

Walking with William Shakespeare

Oversley Wood.

Turn left along an attractive path running through the bluebells just inside the wood. Leave the wood, crossing straight over a bridleway, and keep ahead along a hedged track that becomes a terraced path following the foot of a valley. Keep to the track as it curves left around the hillside crowned by a large white building, Oversley Castle. The track climbs a little to reveal more lovely views and brings you to a T-junction. Turn right, downhill, and follow the track as it weaves around Oversley Farm and meets a narrow lane.

Bear left down the lane for the crossroads at **Wixford.** The Three Horseshoes Inn offers welcome refreshment. The intriguingly-named Crabtree Farm is close by—could there be some truth behind the tale of the drinking contest? Opposite the pub, follow the lane signed for Exhall and Temple Grafton. After about 50 yards, turn left, following the sign for Exhall village. After about half a mile, as you enter the village, look carefully on your right

One of the pretty cottages in Arden's Grafton

for a post with a footpath sign. Take the raised path, which leads you into **St. Giles's churchyard.** The little church dates from the twelfth century. Leave the church on your left, and follow the path through a gate to exit the churchyard. Turn right and keep straight ahead, with a hedge on your right, down a grassy path. Go through a gate and continue over the fields, keeping the hedge on your right. Cross a stile and continue for only a few yards before bearing right over a stream. Keep ahead, still with a hedge on your right. Go over a stile and follow the edge of the field ahead. Two stiles take you through a gap in the hedge. Bear left to resume your original heading with the hedge now on your left. Cross the next stile; now bear half-right up the field to the hedge at the top, and cross the stile by a post with a footpath sign. Over the stile, bear half-left (still uphill) to cross another stile. The tiny hamlet in the valley at your feet has the fascinating name of **Little Britain!**

Follow the path beside a fence on your left to cross a stile to a lane. Turn right to walk up to the charming village of **Arden's Grafton** crowning the hilltop. Turn left and follow the footpath beside the lane through the village. Continue along this pleasant path to return to Temple Grafton.

Little Britain

Starting point
Temple Grafton village is about 5 miles west of
Stratford. Approach from the north via the A422;
from the south via the B439. GR 123 549.

Parking: In the village, near the church.

Public transport
For bus times, contact Welcombe Garages at (01789)
204393.

Length of walk: 6 miles.

Map: Ordnance Survey Explorer Map No. 205.

Refreshments
The Three Horseshoes Inn, Wixford (on the route).
The Blue Boar Inn is about one-half mile northwest
of Temple Grafton.

THE WALK IN BRIEF

L eave Temple Grafton Church on the right; walk up the road. Keep ahead over the crossroads and take the footpath on the right over the fields to cross the stile at the top of Grove Hill. Turn left 100 yards, then right down steps to descend the hillside. Go through a gate and bear half-left to cross a stile at the foot of the hill. Cross the field ahead to a farm track. Turn left to a lane. Turn right three-quarters of a mile, then turn right for Rosehall Farm. Pass the farm, go through a gate, and follow the path to Oversley Wood. Turn left to follow the path just within the wood. Keep straight ahead along a hedged track and follow the track as it curves around the hillside to a T-junction. Turn right downhill. The track leads to a lane. Turn left to Wixford, then turn left (signed Exhall and Temple Grafton). After about 50 yards, turn left to walk to Exhall. Take the raised footpath on the right through the churchyard. Turn right and follow the path with the hedge on your right. The path curves right, over a stream. Keep ahead, with the hedge on your right. When double stiles lead through a gap in the hedge, turn left to resume your original heading (with hedge on left). Cross a stile and bear half-right up the field. Over the next stile, bear half-left and follow the path to a road. Turn right uphill and follow the road to Arden's Grafton. Turn left and continue along the pavement beside the road to return to Temple Grafton.

CHAPTER 5

IN THE COTSWOLDS:
DURSLEY, WOODMANCOTE
AND STINCHCOMBE HILL

What you do
Still betters what is done. When you speak, sweet,
I'd have you do it ever: when you sing,
I'd have you buy and sell so; so give alms;
Pray so; and, for the ord'ring your affairs,
To sing them too: when you do dance, I wish you
A wave o'the sea, that you might ever do
Nothing but that; move still, still so,
And own no other function . . .
—Florizel, *The Winter's Tale*

Shakespeare wrote *The Winter's Tale* in 1610 shortly before he retired. It is a romantic play containing some of his loveliest free-flowing lyrical poetry. But it opens on a harsh note. The King of Bohemia (Polixines) and the King of Sicilia (Leontes) have been friends from childhood. But after a visit from Polixines, Leontes accuses his wife, Hermione, of bearing his former friend's child. Bitterly jealous, he banishes her to prison, and after the baby is born, he orders the little girl to be abandoned. The baby, with a bundle containing gold and some proofs of her identity, is discovered on a beach in Bohemia by a shepherd who brings her up as his daughter, Perdita. When the Delphic oracle proclaims Hermione's innocence, Leontes is overcome with grief and repents. Time passes, and at the sheep-shearing feast Perdita and Prince Florizel, Polixines's son, pledge their love for each other. After some further complications all is soon happily resolved. The young lovers can marry, and Leontes's repentance brings forgiveness and finally reconciliation.

The story has a fairytale quality just right, as its title suggests, for a tale told in the firelight of a winter's evening. The humble shepherdess who is really a princess and eventually wins her Prince Charming has all the perennial appeal of Cinderella. But the play is very far from being dreamlike or whimsical! Shakespeare brings his characters alive and introduces us to real, well-rounded people. This is particularly true of the pastoral scenes, set in the Cotswold Hills. These chalk hills were famous for their great flocks of sheep and the quality of their wool. The sheep-shearing feast, presided over by Perdita, attracts a crowd of instantly recognizable folk. There is the merry rogue Autolycus, that "snapper up of unconsider'd trifles" who tempts the simple country girls with his pedlars' wares. He offers ballads with most unlikely themes. "Is it true, think you?" they ask. One of the girls, Mopsa, has no doubts. "I love a ballad in print, for then we are sure they are true," she assures them. A view that has stood the test of time! The old shepherd is surely an authentic voice as he compares Perdita's shy modesty as queen of the feast with that of his wife when she was alive:

> Fie daughter! When my old wife lived, upon
> This day she was both pantler, butler, cook;
> Both dame and servant; welcomed all; served all;
>
> . . . .
>
> her face o'fire
> With labour and the thing she took to quench it.

Perdita welcomes her guests with flowers, in exquisite verse, but as we would expect from her country upbringing, she is practical and knows her own mind. She considers grafting to be falsifying nature. When Camillo, a disguised courtier impressed by her beauty, tells her,

> I should leave grazing, were I of your flock,
> And only live by gazing,

she replies,

> Out, alas!
> You'd be so lean, that blasts of January
> Would blow you through and through.

There was no need for Shakespeare to invent these people; they were part of his world. He had sat with them at sheep-shearing feasts and enjoyed their saffron cakes and warden pies. (Wardens were a variety of pear.) His father, like many other glovers, dealt in wool. It is possible he traded illegally, as licenses from the London Wool Staple were difficult to obtain. As the eldest boy, William would have accompanied his father on his business trips to the Cotswolds. The deal would be made in early summer and the wool collected in June after the shearing to be resold at a profit in towns and markets. He would have heard the shepherds working out how much to charge for their wool, like the shepherd's son in *The Winter's Tale*: "Let me see: every 'leven wether tods [eleven sheep make one tod, i.e., twenty-eight pounds of wool]; every tod yields pound and odd shilling: fifteen hundred shorn, what comes the wool to? . . . I cannot do't without counters." Apart from enjoying the festivities, the young Shakespeare may have made contacts that were to become very useful in the future.

Between 1582, when Shakespeare married and brought Anne to live in Henley Street, and 1592, when he is known to have been in London, only two other facts in his life are recorded: the christening of Susanna, born in May 1583, and the christening of twins Hamnet and Judith in February 1585. What did he do during those "lost years"? He obviously needed money. He had a young family to support, and his father was losing both his business and his status in the community. Many theories have been proposed, including sending him to sea with Drake in *The Golden Hinde!* The sea plays an important part in several of his plays, but the exploits of English sailors as they fought the French and Spanish and explored new lands must have been a frequent topic of conversation, especially after the defeat of the Armada in 1588. He could have worked in a lawyer's office, as many legal terms find their way into his plays. But suing each other for debt was a favorite occupation among the better-off townsfolk of Stratford, including Shakespeare's father. To find a possible answer, I would like to take you, and Shakespeare, back to the Cotswolds.

The first biographer of Shakespeare was John Aubrey,

The Broadwell stream runs past a quiet corner of Dursley

born in 1626, who included a short account of the poet in his *Brief Lives*. Although his information is not always reliable, his notes on Shakespeare were taken from Christopher Beeston, an actor who died in 1682 and the son of William Beeston, one of Shakespeare's fellow actors. Aubrey states that "Shakespeare understood Latin pretty well: for he had been in his younger days a schoolmaster in the country." Although Shakespeare's fellow playwright Ben Jonson said he had "little Latin and less Greek," Shakespeare's grammar school education would have fitted him well for the task. Jonson was a classical scholar—his knowledge of the classics would be awe-inspiring today—and he frequently enjoyed making critical remarks about his rival.

There is a tradition that Shakespeare taught for a time in Dursley, an old market town beside the river Ewelme, in the shadow of Stinchcombe Hill. The highest hill in the area, Stinchcombe rises at the western edge of the Cotswold escarpment, with magnificent views over the

Berkeley Castle

Vale of Berkeley and the estuary of the river Severn to the Welsh Hills. Dursley and the neighboring village of Woodmancote were centers of the woollen industry famous for their woven broadcloth. Fulling mills, where the cloth was washed and finished, once lined the river.

Shakespeare obviously knew the area well. In *The Second Part of Henry IV*, Justice Shallow has a comfortable house in these hills. When his servant, Davy, asks him, "Shall we sow the headland with wheat?" Shallow replies, "With red wheat, Davy." Red wheat, which could grow on dry soils, was sown on the chalk of the Cotswold Hills until the eighteenth century. Davy asks Justice Shallow to support "William Visor of Woncot" in a court case with "Clement Perkes o'th'hill." Shakespeare used the local pronunciation of Woodmancote, "Woncot," and knew that Stinchcombe Hill was always called "the hill" by the villagers—as it still is today. Church and tax records prove that Clement Perkes and William Visor were real people. The Vizor family (Elizabethan spelling, like Cleopatra, was capable of infinite variety) worked in the woollen industry, and an Arthur Vizor lies buried in Dursley churchyard.

Berkeley Castle stands proudly beside the Severn estuary. The castle features in *Richard II*, and interesting details in the play again suggest that Shakespeare was familiar with the area. Bolingbroke, returning from exile, is crossing the Cotswold Hills with his army on his way to Bristol. He is riding with his ally, the Earl of Northumberland. The king is fighting in Ireland and the Duke of York, acting as regent, has garrisoned Berkeley Castle with the intention of stopping Bolingbroke's progress. From a vantage point in the hills, Bolingbroke reins in his horse to ask the earl, "How far is it, my lord, to Berkeley now?" The earl does not know, but his son, Henry Percy, who joins them a little later, is able to enlighten them. "There stands the castle," he says, adding helpfully, "by yond tuft of trees." When you stand on the crest of Stinchcombe Hill, you will see the same view of Berkeley Castle today, although "the tuft of trees" has grown and obscures part of the building. Did Shakespeare recall standing on the hill when he wrote this scene? Follow the route of this walk, which encircles the summit, and draw your own conclusions!

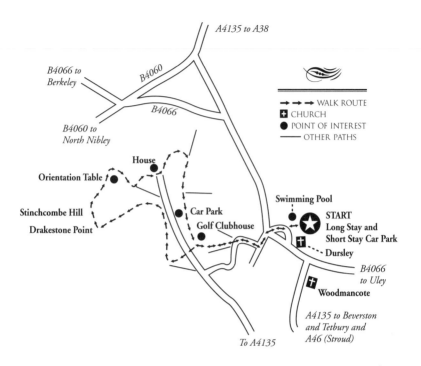

The walk starts from **Dursley**'s long stay car park just past the swimming pool. Leave the entrance to the car park, walk past the adjacent short stay park (keeping the swimming pool building on your right), and cross the A4135 at the traffic lights. Follow the green Cotswold Way sign straight ahead to walk up May Lane past the library on your right. Turn right to climb Hill Road, passing a short stay car park on your left. When Hill Road swings left, follow the footpath straight ahead signed for the Cotswold Way; on the same post, a little to the left, you will see another sign indicating the path to the top of Stinchcombe Hill, which is our destination. Pass a chain, and immediately you are faced with three possible paths. Follow the middle path, which climbs up the side of a beautiful valley through beech woods. The path is steep,

The wonderful view over the Vale of Berkeley and the Severn Estuary from Stinchcombe Hill. Berkeley Castle is in the center of the picture, half-hidden by trees, just in front of the white square of the power station.

and you may find yourself agreeing with the Earl of Northumberland, who moans, "These high wild hills and rough uneven ways / Draw out our miles." But you are soon at the top, rewarded with splendid views!

The path levels to run to the right of a boarded fence and bring you over a stile to the southeast corner of the large grassy plateau on the top of **Stinchcombe Hill**. Shaped like a clover leaf, it is the only extensive area of flat uncultivated land for many miles and is used as a golf course. But there is plenty of space for walkers, too, and many delightful footpaths. When Bolingbroke accepted the Duke of York's invitation to spend the night at Berkeley Castle—the Duke decided his forces were too weak to oppose him—this great plateau would have provided an ideal campsite for his army. Pass the golf clubhouse on your right, and turn left along the track for only a few yards to a Cotswold Way sign pointing southwest across the golf course. Bear right over the grass, as the sign directs, and follow the line of posts marked with yellow arrow footpath signs over the golf course to the woods on the other side.

The tomb of Dickie Pearce in Berkeley churchyard. He was the last "fool" or court jester in England, dying in 1728 aged 63.

Turn right to walk beside the golf course, with the woods descending steeply on your left. Shortly, the trees give way to reveal a wonderful view southwards over the Wiltshire plain. On your left, an outlying spur of the Cotswolds is crowned by a tall pillar in memory of William Tyndale, the first person to translate the Bible into English.

Continue along the hilltop, keeping your height and bearing left to head west to **Drakestone Point**, where a seat provides a welcome opportunity to rest and admire the view. The path then swings north along the western edge of the plateau to another seat before curving a little further north. Follow the path as it rises to bring you to a stone seat; a few yards farther on you come to an orientation table. Here the trees on the western slopes give way to reveal the view of **Berkeley Castle** that I suggest Henry Percy pointed out to Bolingbroke and the Earl of Northumberland. The castle is not easy to see, as most of the building is masked by trees, but it is just to the left of

Walking with William Shakespeare

the tower of Berkeley's village church, directly in line with the off-white square shape of Berkeley Power Station. The direction of the castle (and New York!) is indicated on the orientation table. The castle is only about five miles from Dursley, and it is tempting to imagine that if Shakespeare was teaching in the area, he may have taken time off to ride to the castle to see plays performed by the Earl of Berkeley's Players. He may have known some of the actors already, as they had visited Stratford in 1581 and again in 1583. Perhaps they encouraged this personable young man in his twenties to think about an acting career!

The path leads a short distance downhill to a stone shelter, then climbs to a waymarked post. (The posts throughout the walk are marked with signs for several trails, but just keep your height and continue with the golf course on your right.) Pass a path marked for the Cotswold Way on your right, and keep ahead to cross a road leading to a house in the trees on your left. Keep following the path around the edge of the plateau, turning right to head south back towards the golf clubhouse. Walk past the front of the building, and turn left to retrace your steps over the stile and follow the path downhill to **Dursley**. Find time if you can to explore this delightful little town with its elegant Georgian houses and picturesque Market House. The bells of the five-hundred-year-old church of St. James ring a carillon every three hours, playing a different hymn each day of the week.

In our next chapter, we leave the peace of the hills to follow Shakespeare into a different world.

The brightly painted medieval chancel screen in Berkeley church

Starting point and parking

Dursley long stay car park. Dursley is beside the A4135, midway between Bristol and Gloucester. Turn for Dursley off the A38 or approach via the M5 leaving at junctions 13 or 14. The car park is off Castle Street just past the large swimming pool building. GR 756 982.

Public transport

There are regular bus services from Bristol and Gloucester. For times, contact Traveline at (0870) 608 2 608.

Length of walk

4.5 miles. This includes a steep climb; if you wish, you can avoid the climb and drive up Hill Road to the car park on the top of Stinchcombe Hill.

Map

Ordnance Survey Explorer Map No. 167.

Refreshments

Cafes, pubs and restaurants in Dursley.

From the long stay car park, leave the swimming pool building on your right, cross the A4135 at the lights, continue straight ahead (Cotswold Way sign) along May Lane, and turn right up Hill Lane. When Hill Lane swings left, follow the footpath ahead past a chain. Take the middle path of the three paths ahead, and follow it uphill over a stile to the golf clubhouse on the top of Stinchcombe Hill. Turn left for a few yards, then bear right over the grass, following the Cotswold Way sign. The path is indicated by posts with yellow arrows. Cross the road and continue to the woods. Turn right along the edge of the plateau. Follow one of the footpaths, keeping your height, around the plateau, which is shaped like a clover leaf. Do not miss the orientation table and the magnificent view over the Vale of Berkeley! When you return to the clubhouse, leave the building on your left and turn left to retrace your steps over the stile, downhill to Dursley.

CHAPTER 6

AN "UPSTART CROW":
EARLY DAYS IN LONDON

They say this town is full of cozenage;
As, nimble jugglers that do deceive the eye,
Dark-working sorcerers that change the mind,
Soul-killing witches that deform the body,
Disguised cheaters, prating mountebanks,

. . . .

I greatly fear my money is not safe.
—Antipholus of Syracuse, *The Comedy of Errors*

P erhaps this was the warning Shakespeare received from the more knowledgeable in Stratford when he mentioned he might leave his parents and young family to seek his fortune in London as an actor. This was a brave decision for him to make, but it was not without precedent. Everyone knew the story of Hugh Clopton, who, in the mid-fifteenth century, rode from Stratford to London, became Lord Mayor, and returned to his native town to build a fine bridge (still in use today) over the Avon and an impressive house, New Place. Another young man from Stratford, Richard Field, had apprenticed himself to a London printer, Thomas Vautrollier. When Thomas died, Richard married his widow and was now running one of the best printing houses in the city. He printed Shakespeare's first published works, two long poems (*Venus and Adonis* in April 1593 and *The Rape of Lucrece* in 1594), probably under the poet's supervision. So Shakespeare would not find himself friendless when he arrived in the great city.

But why did Shakespeare decide to leave his home, abandoning perhaps the schoolmaster's desk or the lawyer's office? There is some support for the tradition that he fled to escape the wrath of Sir Thomas Lucy of Charlecote, whose deer he had been poaching, but John Aubrey, with his keen ear for gossip, does not mention it in his *Brief Lives* and Charlecote had no deer park. Nor do I believe, as has been suggested, that Shakespeare, with his good sense and cautious nature, would have left for London on a whim and been discovered standing in the yard looking after playgoers' horses. I believe he made the decision to be an actor because he fell in love with the life. Players' companies visited Stratford regularly, and perhaps he awaited an opportunity to join one of them. Self-confident, handsome and musical, he probably felt he stood a good chance of success in the new, exciting world of professional theater.

Acting was not new. Mystery and morality plays were popular throughout the Middle Ages, but they were performed by tradesmen who did not expect to get paid, nor did people expect to pay to watch them. But by the beginning of Elizabeth's reign, there was a growing public demand for plays with secular themes to be performed by groups of professionals. An Act of 1572 had classified "Common Players" as rogues and vagabonds unless they could obtain the patronage of a baron or other "honorable Personage." The Lord Mayor and Corporation of the City of London disliked the players, fearing the crowds gathering to watch plays could lead to riots. But their jurisdiction held only within the city limits. Beyond their control were rapidly growing suburbs known as "liberties" where players were generally welcome. And the queen enjoyed plays and wished to have well-practiced actors to amuse her at court. In 1574 she overruled the corporation of the Puritan-led city of London and issued a royal patent authorizing the Earl of Leicester's men to perform plays, with the approval of the Master of the Revels, "as well within our City of London and Liberties of the same as elsewhere." In 1583 she formed her own company of players, the Queen's Men, and assigned them two inns as "Playing Places" within the city: the Bull in Bishopsgate and the Bell in Gracious [Gracechurch] Street. As well as performances in her royal palaces, plays were also performed in the great halls of the Inns of Court before an audience of law students composed of the sons of the landed gentry and the rising middle class, and in the grand homes of the nobility.

And the Queen's Men now had a real purpose-built playhouse. Earlier, in 1576, James Burbage, one of Leicester's men, had obtained a twenty-one-year lease and permission to build the first public playhouse on land just north of Bishopsgate in the parish of St. Leonard's, in the

splendid bust of Shakespeare on the site of St. Mary's Church in Love Lane. Shakespeare had lodgings ... ...y. His friends Heminge and Condell, who compiled the First Folio of his plays, also lived in the parish.

Liberty of Holywell, Shoreditch. It was called simply the Theatre. Another playhouse, the Curtain, was built close by, and in 1585 Philip Henslowe, a wealthy moneylender, built the Rose on Bankside in the Liberty of the Clink across the river in Southwark.

The playhouses were modelled on the galleried inn yards where plays were traditionally performed. Half-timbered walls, infilled with lath and plaster, surrounded an area of about a hundred feet across. An apron or platform stage projected into the yard, where it was surrounded on three sides by the "groundlings" who stood in the open throughout the performance. Entry to the yard cost a penny. For those willing to spend a penny or two more, there were seats, some comfortably padded, in the three tiers of galleries. At the back of the stage was the tiring house—the actors' dressing rooms—with doors on either side opening onto the stage. Between them was a recess with another door and possibly a curtain. The middle gallery ran behind the stage, forming the box, or Lord's Room, where wealthy patrons would see little of the action but could show off their finery. It also could be used by musicians. The upper gallery continued above this. From the top, a roof (known as the shadow) supported by pillars projected across part of the stage. A hut surmounted the tiring house. A flag was hoisted and trumpets sounded to announce a performance. The building was well-planned and versatile. Performances were continuous, utilizing three possible acting areas: the projecting apron stage, the inner stage or recess (useful for plays demanding small set scenes such as caves or studies), and the box above, which could serve as battlements or balconies. But its greatest asset was its intimacy: nothing divided actors and audience. Everyone could feel they were part of the action.

So when Shakespeare weighed up his chances of success in London in his chosen profession, he knew he would find an eager and receptive audience, possibly noisy at times as they munched apples and cracked nuts, but used to listening attentively and reacting warmly to the spoken word. He knew people from all levels of society were willing to pay for the privilege of hearing plays. This fact would not be lost on Shakespeare, who throughout his life combined genius with shrewd business sense. Already the way had been paved by a group of playwrights known as the "University Wits" who had written plays modelled on classical drama. Audiences were thrilling to Christopher Marlowe's majestic "mighty line" in *Tamberlaine*.

The date when Shakespeare left Stratford is not known, but I think he would have been reluctant to leave before the birth of his twins in 1585. In the winter of 1587, the most prestigious company of actors, the Queen's Men, visited Stratford. They were fine actors, sworn servants of the queen, wearing scarlet liveries as grooms of the chamber. And when they arrived, this dazzling company was a man short. One of their number, William Knell, had been killed by a fellow actor at Thame. Here was an opportunity for Shakespeare to take his place, and it is likely he joined the company in the rather lowly status as a "hired man," returning with them to London to entertain the queen at Greenwich.

By 1592 he had been in London long enough to write several plays so successful that they aroused the jealousy of the playwright Robert Greene. As one of the University Wits, Greene attributed the success of this grammar school boy from the provinces to imitation of the work of his betters. On his deathbed he wrote a pamphlet called *Greene's Groats-worth of Wit, bought with a Million of Repentance* in which he attacked Shakespeare, calling him "an upstart Crow, beautified with our feathers, that with his *Tygers hart wrapt in a Players hyde,* supposes he is as well able to bombast out a blank verse as the best of you: and being an absolute *Johannes factotum,* is in his own conceit the only Shake-scene in the country." In this attack Greene quotes a line from Shakespeare's *The Third Part of Henry VI,* substituting "Players" for "woman's," and uses italics to make his meaning doubly clear. The pamphlet was printed by Henry Chettle. Evidently there were some objections, and Chettle published an apology. He had, he wrote, been approached by "divers of worship" [important people] who had praised Shakespeare's "uprightness of dealing, which argues his honesty, and his facetious [stylish] grace in writing, that approves his Art." Thanks to Greene's spite, we know that Shakespeare had already gained favor among influential people.

The most successful of these early plays was a superb trilogy of history plays based on the life of Henry VI. Shakespeare was always aware of his audience, and in choosing history as his theme, he seized the mood of the moment. After the defeat of the Armada in 1588, a wave of patriotism swept the country. There was renewed interest in the country's past, the legitimacy of the Tudors' claim to the throne had to be supported, and all plays were censored. Henry VI's inability to control his ambitious nobles had led to the horrors of the Wars of the Roses, with the houses of York and Lancaster fighting for supremacy. The wars were brought to an end by the defeat of the Yorkist Richard III at Bosworth by the Earl of Richmond, who, as Henry VII, inaugurated the Tudor dynasty. Henry's claim to the throne (he was the son of Margaret Beaufort, great-granddaughter of John of Gaunt, fourth son of Edward III) could be contested. His granddaughter, Queen Elizabeth I, was popular, but she had many enemies eager to support rival claimants. So Shakespeare, taking his facts from the historian Holinshed, who favored the Tudor view of history, was on safe ground. Swift-moving action and frequent battle scenes ensured the attention of the less politically minded in his audience.

The *Henry VI* trilogy already reveals Shakespeare's mastery of blank verse. It is full of splendid poetry. But it reveals also another aspect of his genius that distinguishes him from Marlowe and other dramatists of the time. Unlike his rivals, he understood and sympathized with the complexity of human nature. His Henry is recognizably real, foolish but innocent. He wins our sympathy as, dismissed as useless from the battlefield, he sits down on a molehill (a homely touch—so typical of Shakespeare) wishing he had been a simple shepherd rather than a king:

> Gives not the hawthorn bush a sweeter shade
> To shepherds looking on their silly sheep,
> Than doth a rich-embroider'd canopy
> To kings that fear their subjects' treachery?
> O, yes, it doth; a thousand-fold it doth.

In *Richard III*, another early play, Shakespeare follows Holinshed and draws a picture of a ruthless villain determined to be a villain and gain the crown by destroying all in his path. Lies and deceit are second nature to Richard. Yet even Richard has his moments of self-doubt. Before Bosworth he suffers a dreadful night when the ghosts of all whom he has wronged condemn him. He wakes, crying, "O coward conscience, how dost thou afflict me!" He has the courage to recognize himself for what he is and has no illusions as he concludes:

> I shall despair. There is no creature loves me;
> And if I die, no soul will pity me:
> Nay, wherefore should they, since that I myself
> Find in myself no pity to myself?

While writing these early plays, Shakespeare was probably

involved with several companies of players, including Lord Strange's Men. In March 1592 Henslowe records in his diary a performance by them of *The First Part of Henry VI* at his theater, the Rose. It is possible they put on performances at Burbage's Theatre in spring and autumn, and in one of the city inns during winter. Where Shakespeare may have lodged during these early days is not known, but it is possible he lived close to the Theatre in Holywell Lane. In *Brief Lives*, John Aubrey notes that Shakespeare "lived in Shoreditch" for a time. Evidently Shakespeare relied on hard work as well as talent, as Aubrey adds he was "the more to be admired because he was not a company-keeper," and he "wouldn't be debauched [made drunk] and, if invited to, writ—he was in pain." Shakespeare's first known address is in the parish of St. Helen's, Bishopsgate, where tax records place him between 1592 and 1596. For our first walk in London, we will follow him there and also visit some other places Shakespeare would have known north of the Thames.

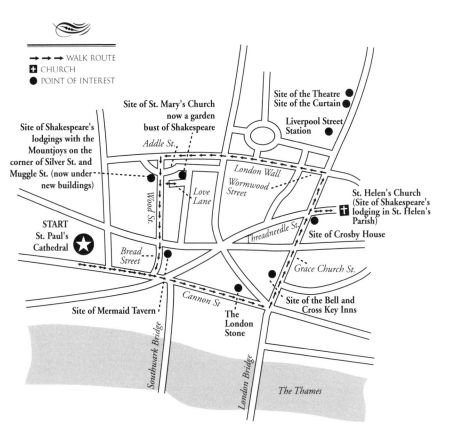

We start the walk from **St. Paul's Cathedral.** In Shakespeare's day, before the Great Fire of 1666 resulted in the building of Christopher Wren's masterpiece, this was a huge Gothic church standing high on Ludgate Hill, dominating the southwest corner of the old walled city. It was the center of London literary life, and the surrounding churchyard was filled with printers' shops and bookstalls. Here Shakespeare carefully supervised the printing of *Venus and Adonis* by Richard Field, and copies could be bought "at the signe of the white Greyhound in Paules Church-yard." The playbook of

Twelfth-century St. Helen's Church in Bishopsgate. In 1596 Shakespeare lodged nearby.

Shakespeare's *Troilus and Cressida* was for sale "at the Spread Eagle at Paul's Churchyard over against the great North Door."

Leave the cathedral on your left and head east along the southern branch of the churchyard to the junction with Cannon Street. Keep straight on along the left-hand side of Cannon Street to cross Queen Street and continue until you see Cannon Street Station across the road. Opposite the station, just above pavement level on your left, you will see a remnant of the **London Stone** set in the wall behind a grille. The stone has been removed from an earlier site and its origins are obscure, but Shakespeare makes use of it in *The Second Part of Henry VI*. Jack Cade, pretending to have royal connections as Mortimer, leads his rebel army over London Bridge intending to storm the city. He strikes his staff on the London Stone, then sits on it proclaiming, "Now is Mortimer lord of this city. And here, sitting upon London-stone, I charge and command that . . . the pissing-conduit run nothing but claret wine. . . ."

Continue down Cannon Street, cross King William Street, and turn left up **Gracechurch Street.** In Shakespeare's day this was the main road leading north out of the city and south to the only bridge across the Thames, London Bridge. As you walk up the street, you will find that the memory of the inns where his plays were performed lives on in some of the place names. On the left you pass **Bell Inn Yard.** The Bell was one of the inns chosen by the queen for her players. A plaque on the wall of the entrance to the yard states that this was also the site of the Cross Keys Inn, another favorite "Playing Place." Continue up Gracechurch Street, which becomes Bishopsgate after you cross Cornhill. Follow Bishopsgate to the junction with Threadneedle Street. Crosby House, where Richard III lodged as Duke of Gloucester, once stood on the right-hand side of Bishopsgate opposite the junction. In the play, he bids his wife-to-be, Lady Anne, to "presently repair to Crosby House." Turn right down Great St. Helen's, a passageway leading to **St. Helen's Church,** which dates from the twelfth century. This beautiful church retains its medieval charm and contains memorials to many eminent citizens, including John Crosby, who built the house of the same name. St. Helen's was Shakespeare's parish church in 1596 when he lodged nearby. He would have worshipped here on Sundays and often walked past the church on his way to the Theatre in Shoreditch or one of the inns in Gracechurch Street. He is commemorated in a stained glass window presented by H. H. Prentice of the United States in 1884.

Return to Bishopsgate and turn right to head north as far as the junction with Wormwood Street on your left. Shakespeare, on his way to the Theatre, would have kept straight on through Bishopsgate to leave the walled city and continue to Shoreditch. Nothing remains of the

Theatre or the Curtain. Only two street names, Curtain Road and Holywell Lane, recall their existence. Turn left along Wormwood Street and keep ahead as the street becomes London Wall to cross Moorgate. As you approach the Barbican buildings you come to Wood Street, signed on the left for St. Paul's Station. Turn left down Wood Street, passing Addle Street on your left. Take the next left turn, Love Lane, and after a few yards (just before the junction with Aldermanbury) there is a small **garden** on your left. Dominating the garden is a fine **bust of Shakespeare.** From 1602 until possibly 1606 he lodged nearby with Christopher and Mary Mountjoy on the corner of Silver Street and Muggle Street. The entrance to Silver Street was opposite Addle Street, but the whole area on the west side of Wood Street has disappeared under modern buildings. The bust once stood outside his parish church, St. Mary's. The church was badly damaged by bombs during the last war and the romantic ruin has been carefully dismantled and taken across the Atlantic to Westminster College in Fulton, Missouri, where it has been restored as a memorial for Winston Churchill. The garden was made on the site of the church. Shakespeare's friends John Heminge and Henry Condell, who collected and edited the First Folio of his plays, are commemorated on the plinth supporting the bust. They also lived nearby and were buried in the church.

One reminder of how part of this area once looked is a surviving stretch of the **London Wall.** To see the wall, retrace your steps to Wood Street, then turn left for a few feet to walk along St. Alban's Court to the garden on the site of St. Mary Staining Church. With the garden on your right, follow Oat Lane to a T-junction. The wall is directly in front of you.

Retrace your steps to Wood Street, and turn right to walk down to the junction with Cheapside. Cross the road to the corner of Bread Street. The Mermaid Tavern once stood on this corner. It was the home of the Friday Street Club founded by Sir Walter Raleigh. Shakespeare and Ben Jonson were members. In his *Worthies of England*, published in 1662, Thomas Fuller describes how Shakespeare and Jonson engaged in battles of wit "like a Spanish great galleon and an English man-of-war; Master Jonson . . . was built far higher in learning, solid but slow in his performances. Shakespeare . . . lesser in bulk, but lighter in sailing, could turn with all tides, tack about and take advantage of all winds. . . ."

Walk down Bread Street to Cannon Street and turn right to retrace your steps to St. Paul's Cathedral. In 1592 the outlook was bright for Shakespeare. But suddenly everything was to change and he would have need of his ability to "take advantage of all winds."

*St. Helen's Church was Shakespeare's parish church in 1596. The
stained glass window bearing his portrait was given to St. Helen's by
H. H. Prentice in 1884.*

Starting Point: St. Paul's Cathedral.

Nearest Tube Station: St. Paul's.

Length of walk: 4 miles.

Map
Supplement my sketch map with a good London city
map.

St. Helen's Church is closed on Saturdays.

H ead east along the southern branch of St. Paul's churchyard and continue along Cannon Street. Opposite Cannon Street Station, the London Stone is set in the wall on your left. Turn left up Gracechurch Street, note the sites of the Bell and Cross Keys inns, and continue up Bishopsgate to the junction with Threadneedle Street. Crosby House once stood on the corner on the right-hand side of Bishopsgate. Turn right down Great St. Helen's to the church. Shakespeare lived for a time in St. Helen's parish. Return to Bishopsgate and continue to the junction with Wormwood Street. Turn left along Wormwood Street and London Wall as far as the Barbican buildings. Turn left just before them along Wood Street, then left along Love Lane. On the left, note the fine bust of Shakespeare on the site of the former church of St. Mary, now replaced by a garden. Shakespeare had lodgings nearby in Silver Street, which ran west opposite Addle Street but is now built over. Part of the old London Wall survives. To see it, return to Wood Street and turn left down St. Alban's Court. Pass the site of St. Mary Staining Church and follow Oat Lane to a T-junction. Cross the road to the wall, which is directly opposite. Return to Wood Street and turn right. Walk down Wood and cross Cheapside to Bread Street. The Mermaid Tavern, noted for battles of wit between Shakespeare and Ben Jonson, once stood on the corner. Walk down Bread Street to Cannon Street and turn right to return to St. Paul's Cathedral.

CHAPTER 7

POETRY AND PATRONAGE:
WITH THE EARL OF SOUTHAMPTON AT TITCHFIELD

Shall I compare thee to a summer's day?
Thou art more lovely and more temperate.
Rough winds do shake the darling buds of May,
And summer's lease hath all too short a date.
Sometime too hot the eye of heaven shines,
And often is his gold complexion dimmed;
And every fair from fair sometime declines,
By chance, or nature's changing course, untrimmed;

But thy eternal summer shall not fade,
Nor lose possession of that fair thou ow'st
Nor shall Death brag thou wand'rest in his shade,
When in eternal lines to time thou grow'st.
So long as men can breathe or eyes can see,
So long lives this, and this gives life to thee.

—Sonnet 18

In his plays we have to look for Shakespeare behind the mask of his characters, but in his sonnets we find the man himself. Such an intense and frank portrayal of love in all its aspects could be drawn only from firsthand experience. Shakespeare followed Philip Sydney's advice to look in his heart and write. His sonnets have become the most famous love poems in our language, but if the players' companies had not suffered a serious setback in 1592 they might never have been written!

By late summer of that year, Shakespeare's plays were rivalling those of Marlowe. Then disaster struck. Outbreaks of plague were not uncommon, but at the end of September plague deaths in London reached epidemic proportions. To avoid infection, the playhouses were closed. They remained closed until the beginning of December, opened briefly for the Christmas season, then closed again until June 1594. Deprived of their income, the players' companies could not survive. The Queen's Men were losing their dominance, playing only once at court in 1591 while Lord Strange's Company played six times. It is possible Shakespeare could have been with Strange's company who, unable to use their London theaters, applied to the Privy Council for a new license giving them leave to travel. But when this was granted in May 1593, it named Edward Alleyn, William Kempe, Thomas Pope, John Heminge, Augustine Phillips, and George Bryan. There was no mention of Shakespeare. We do not hear of him again until March 1595, when his name appears in the accounts of the queen's treasurer along with those of Kempe and Richard Burbage as payees for plays performed at Greenwich the previous Christmas. Early in 1594, possibly before Shakespeare joined them, Strange's men had formed a new company under the patronage of Lord Chamberlain Hunsdon. Shakespeare would have fared no better if, as is also possible, he had been with other groups of players. The most likely is the company performing under the patronage of the Earl of Pembroke. But in 1592 they were forced to disband, sell their costumes, and go home.

So Shakespeare had to be quick off the mark. He was a married man with three children. If he could not earn money in the playhouse, he would have to find another way to use his poetic gifts. To succeed he needed a rich and influential patron who would, he hoped, provide monetary support and social advancement. He chose a member of one of the noblest families in England: Henry Wriothesley, third Earl of Southampton and Baron of Titchfield. At the age of eighteen, this well-educated, extremely handsome young man was a patron of the arts and already a favorite with the queen. Choosing his theme from his beloved Ovid's *Metamorphoses*, Shakespeare wrote a long erotic poem, *Venus and Adonis*, in which the goddess of love tries in vain to seduce the handsome but cold-hearted Adonis. She pleads with him to enter the "ivory pale" of her arms:

I'll be a park, and thou shalt be my deer:
Feed where thou wilt, on mountain or in dale;

> Graze on my lips, and if those hills be dry,
> Stray lower, where the pleasant fountains lie.

The poem was registered at Stationers' Hall on April 19, 1593, and dedicated to the earl with the kind of self-deprecating address that would be expected of a commoner. Shakespeare could only hope this first offering would please the earl and win him a patron. The poem, with its sensual and titillating theme, richly decorated with the imagery and clever phrasing so popular with the Elizabethans, was an immediate success. It was received with raptures in well-bred and aristocratic circles. The young men of the universities and Inns of Court declared they would "worship sweet Mr Shakespeare," put his portrait on the walls of their rooms, and sleep with *Venus and Adonis* under their pillows. The young earl was evidently pleased. When Shakespeare dedicated a "graver work," *The Rape of Lucrece*, to him the following year, he felt able to address him with the confidence of a friend: "The warrant I have of your honourable disposition, not the worth of my untutored lines makes it assured of acceptance. . . ." Like *Venus and Adonis*, Lucrece was popular for the sensual quality of the verse:

> Her lily hand her rosy cheek lies under,
> Cozening the pillow of a lawful kiss;
> Who, therefore angry, seems to part in sunder,
> Swelling on either side to want his bliss.

A close relationship was developing between Shakespeare, ever responsive to beauty, and the brilliant young earl surrounded by a cultured and glamorous circle of friends and admirers. Flattered by the praise showered on him as the patron of so gifted a poet as Shakespeare (no longer a mere writer of plays, which were not considered

The ruins of Place House, once the Earl of Southampton's main country residence at Titchfield in Hampshire

literature), the earl would surely wish to attach him to his household. The plague would have driven the Southamptons out of their great house in Holborn in London, and they would have taken up residence at their main country home near the village of Titchfield in Hampshire. Known as Palace House, later Place House, this was a splendid mansion standing in a commanding position beside the river Meon, not far from the coast between Portsmouth and Southampton.

The house had been built in 1542 by the earl's grandfather, Thomas Wriothesley, later first Earl of Southampton, around the ruins of a fourteenth-century abbey. When Henry VIII broke away from the Catholic Church in 1532, the monarch destroyed church buildings and seized most of the church land. Thomas Wriothesley had served Henry faithfully as his secretary during the troubled times of his divorce from Catherine of Aragon and

Walking with William Shakespeare

was given the ruined abbey as a reward. After the acceptance of *Venus and Adonis* (possibly circulated in manuscript before being printed), I feel it is very likely Shakespeare spent the plague year of 1593 at the Titchfield mansion, quickly learning the courtly language, ways, and manners that he portrayed in *Love's Labour's Lost*, and writing his early sonnets urging the young earl to marry.

Shakespeare does not name "the lovely boy" of the sonnets, but the earl seems to be the most likely candidate. His father had died in 1581 and he succeeded to the title, his elder brother being already dead. He was the only son of a great house, and, with plague ever present, it was necessary he should marry and produce an heir. He had been placed under the wardship of the powerful Lord Burghley. Wardship amongst Elizabethan rich aristocrats had some surprising connotations. Lord Burghley had the right to choose his ward's bride. For political reasons he insisted the Earl of Southampton should marry his granddaughter Lady Elizabeth Vere. But the eighteen-year-old earl was in no mood to marry. He wanted to follow his hero, the dashing Earl of Essex, share his adventures, and win glory in war. It would have been an advantageous marriage. The Southamptons were Catholics, and marriage with the Protestant Lady Elizabeth would have brought security. In an attempt to impoverish the earl into submission, Burghley could by law penalize the earl with a fine. He imposed the enormous fine of five thousand pounds, but Southampton paid this amount rather than marry. The parallel with Shakespeare's Adonis was obvious, a similarity that possibly occurred to the earl's mother. Perhaps she felt a hint to her son from the poet might help matters!

The earl was fair, a feature Shakespeare stresses in the sonnets, with long golden hair the color, the poet tells us, of marjoram. He had inherited his mother's good looks.

Shakespeare writes:

> Thou art thy mother's glass, and she in thee
> Calls back the lovely April of her prime.

Some authorities have suggested that Shakespeare's "lovely boy" was Lord William Herbert, later Earl of Pembroke, one of the "most noble and incomparable brethren" to whom the First Folio of Shakespeare's plays was dedicated. When the entire sonnet sequence was published by an adventurous bookseller, Thomas Thorpe, in 1609, he dedicated them "To the Onlie Begetter of These Insuing Sonnets Mr W. H. . . ." The initials are right, but Pembroke was only fifteen in 1595, he was not the sole hope of his house (having a father and a brother) so it was not so urgent that he should marry, and he was dark. To support his claim, the sonnets would have to be dated later, and there are convincing verbal parallels between Shakespeare's early plays written between 1593 and 1594 and the early sonnets. In *The Two Gentlemen of Verona*, written in 1594, Proteus remarks:

> Yet writers say: as in the sweetest bud
> The eating canker dwells. . . .

This is echoed in two sonnets:

> And loathsome canker lives in sweetest bud.

and

> For canker vice the sweetest buds doth love.

In another sonnet we read:

> And when a woman woos, what woman's son
> Will sourly leave her till she have prevailed?

This almost repeats the lines from *Venus and Adonis*:

> Art thou a woman's son, and canst not feel
> What 'tis to love, how want of love tormenteth?

In some of his sonnets, Shakespeare fears a rival poet is stealing Southampton's favor. Although Christopher Marlowe's long erotic poem *Hero and Leander*, the most successful of poems based on a story from Ovid, was not published until 1598, it circulated in manuscript before his death in 1593. Shakespeare read and admired Marlowe's poetry, quoting the famous line from *Hero and Leander*, "Who ever loved, that loved not at first sight?" in *As You Like It*. The rival poet had obviously won Shakespeare's respect, as he refers in a sonnet to "the proud full sail of his great verse." He must have been a fine poet to receive such a generous tribute in such difficult circumstances, and I feel only Marlowe could deserve such praise.

But it would have been unthinkable for either earl to be addressed as "Mr."! I favor the explanation that "Mr. W. H." was Sir William Harvey, third husband of the earl's mother. She died in 1607, leaving "the most part of her stuff" to her husband. He was interested in literature, and in looking through her papers he may have come across the sonnets. Thinking they were too good to be hidden away in a drawer, he gave them to Thorpe to be printed. Harvey was only a knight and there was nothing improper in addressing him as "Mr." in its original meaning of "Master." If Sir William is "Mr. W. H.," then in the dedication Thorpe is using "Begetter" in the sense of "procurer."

The gentle urging to marry in the earlier sonnets gives way to a passionate declaration of love as Shakespeare falls victim to the earl's radiant personality. He hails his patron as:

> Lord of my love, to whom in vassalage
> Thy merit hath my duty strongly knit.

With touching openness Shakespeare reveals the depth of this love, his despair when his beloved is absent, and the crushing sense of his social inferiority. Although Shakespeare describes the earl as having a woman's face and gentle heart, their relationship is not sexual, as one of the sonnets makes clear:

> Nature as she wrought thee fell a-doting,
> And by addition me of thee defeated,
> By adding one thing to my purpose nothing
> But since she pricked thee out for women's pleasure,
> Mine be thy love, and thy love's use their treasure.

This difficult relationship becomes more painful after a rival poet appears on the scene and Shakespeare falls in love with a mysterious Dark Lady. It becomes increasingly obvious that she is also the earl's mistress. Although suffering acutely, the poet accepts the situation and tries to believe her when she denies it. He is torn between his desire for her and disgust as he recognizes her power over him:

> Th'expense of spirit in a waste of shame
> Is lust in action. . . .

The whole sonnet sequence was probably completed before 1598, as in that year Francis Meres referred to Shakespeare's "sugar'd sonnets" circulating "among his private friends." But the Dark Lady had entered

Church Street in Titchfield leading to St. Peter's Church

Shakespeare's life much earlier; possibly she was among the earl's acquaintances at Titchfield. *Love's Labour's Lost* displays all the wooing games of a court in a country retreat. Shakespeare, I suggest, wrote this lyrical drama with its puns, witticisms and swift repartee for a small, highly educated audience: the kind of audience he would find at Titchfield. G. P. V. Akrigg, in his *Shakespeare and the Earl of Southampton*, points out that a "play-house room" on the now demolished second floor of the mansion is marked on an eighteenth-century plan.

In *Love's Labour's Lost*, the Dark Lady makes her first appearance. The story revolves around the Princess of France who, accompanied by her three maids of honor, is visiting the King of Navarre. The king falls in love with the princess, and three of the king's courtiers—Berowne, Longaville, and Dumaine—fall in love with the maids. Berowne, often identified with Shakespeare, is attracted, much to his amazement, to Rosaline, "the worst of all," whom he describes as:

> A whitely wanton with a velvet brow,
> With two pitch-balls stuck in her face for eyes.

Those pitch balls were to become the "mourning eyes" of the lady in the sonnets. On the strength of having danced with her once, Berowne is able to declare for no apparent reason that his dark lady is:

> one that will do the deed
> Though Argus were her eunuch and her guard.

She may well ask, with some indignation, for proof of this attack on her morals! Incidentally, the Southampton family regarded *Love's Labour's Lost* as their play and entertained James I's wife—Anne of Denmark—with a performance at their London house in Holborn in January 1605.

In *Romeo and Juliet*, written in 1595, Romeo has sighed for another lady before he met Juliet. She is also called Rosaline. We never meet her, but Mercutio reminds Romeo of his former love and again, for no reason, we have a long description of her attractions. Rosaline is a "pale hard-hearted wench," and he tells us that Romeo has been "stabb'd with a white wench's black eye." At Titchfield the affair with the Dark Lady may have just been a mild flirtation. It was to become much more serious as the later sonnets reveal.

Shakespeare's sonnets were not published until 1609, when he was on the verge of retiring to New Place, the large house he had bought in Stratford. By 1609 Shakespeare was famous, and any new work by him that appeared on the bookstalls should have sold well. But surprisingly, the number of copies sold was small and there was only one printing. The sonnets were not to appear in print again until 1640, safely after Shakespeare's death in 1616. What could be the explanation? Shakespeare had seen his earlier poems carefully through the press, but although the sonnets had a fair text, they contained several errors and it seems unlikely he supervised their printing. If, as I suggested, they were given to Thomas Thorpe by William Harvey, Shakespeare may not have authorized their publication (authors had no automatic copyright at that time) or even known about it. Writing about a passion for a mysterious brunette or a golden-haired young man in sonnets to be privately shown to a few chosen aristocrats would be very different from having them published for the whole country to read. Presumably Shakespeare in 1609 was looking forward to a peaceful retirement with his wife, Anne, and whatever she knew about his life away from Stratford, it is unlikely he would want to embarrass her in print. Even if Anne was not able to read, small-town gossip would soon set her wondering what her William had been up to in London! So it is possible the book was withdrawn from publication before news of its contents could spread to Stratford. Another explanation could be that such a frank revelation of Southampton's affair with the Dark Lady might prove embarrassing at court—if not to him, possibly to the lady. Imagine the gossip! After the accession of James I, Southampton had been released from the Tower and had become one of the king's favorites. Could Shakespeare have had a polite but firm word in Thomas Thorpe's ear?

Today the great house built by the first Earl of Southampton at Titchfield is in ruins. But the imposing gatehouse flanked by four octagonal towers that the earl built across the nave of the former abbey church remains as a reminder of its former glory. Tudor brickwork blends with the pale golden stone of the abbey ruins, and twisted Tudor chimneys rise above walls open to the sky but still retaining their large windows with stone mullions and arched fireplaces. Low walls are all that remain of the range of buildings that once surrounded the large courtyard, originally the abbey cloister. Marked on the ground are the outlines of the rest of the abbey, including the entrance to the chapter house, where the day-to-day business of the abbey was carried out, and the library, once stocked with over a thousand handwritten works.

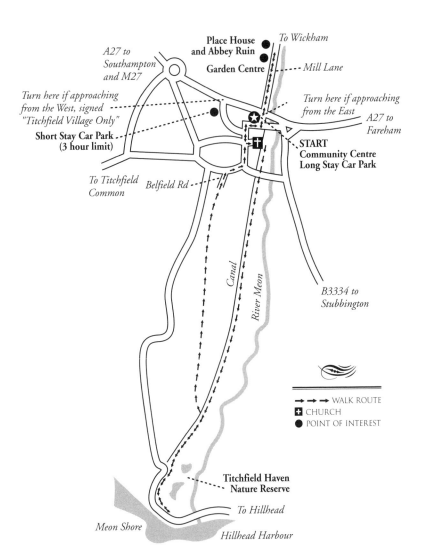

To Wickham

Place House
and Abbey Ruin

Garden Centre

A27 to
Southampton
and M27

Mill Lane

Turn here if approaching
from the West, signed
"Titchfield Village Only"

Turn here if approaching
from the East

A27 to
Fareham

Short Stay Car Park
(3 hour limit)

START
Community Centre
Long Stay Car Park

To Titchfield
Common

Belfield Rd

Canal

River Meon

B3334 to
Stubbington

WALK ROUTE

CHURCH

POINT OF INTEREST

Titchfield Haven
Nature Reserve

To Hillhead

Meon Shore

Hillhead Harbour

T his walk begins with a visit to the ruins of Place
House. Then a lovely ramble along the tow path of
a canal, built by the third Earl of Southampton in
1611, takes us to the sea. Across the Solent rise the downs
of the Isle of Wight and the famous offshore chalk stacks

known as The Needles. If, as I believe, Shakespeare did come to Titchfield, he would have enjoyed the same view, but instead of pleasure yachts and oil tankers he would have seen the tall masts of warships! The Armada launched by France and Spain had been defeated in 1588, but England was still under threat of invasion.

Having parked your car in the Community Centre car park in **Titchfield**, return to the car park entrance and turn left along Mill Street to the A27. Cross the road by the pedestrian crossing at the traffic lights and walk straight ahead along Mill Lane. Pass the entrance to the Abbey Garden Centre; a few yards farther on, turn left through an arch to see the remains of **Place House** and the **former abbey** set among smooth lawns. In 1542 the traveller John Leland described Southampton's home as "a right stateley house, embateled and having a goodely gate." You are free to wander at will and, as the gatehouse has retained its original wooden doors, it is possible that Shakespeare entered by them, too.

When Shakespeare was at Titchfield, his patron was only eighteen. The young earl enjoyed all forms of sport, but one of his favorite pastimes was playing bowls. This was a game usually played by the upper classes. There was a bowling green on the grounds, and the earl is known to have played on Tuesdays and Thursdays. Interestingly, Shakespeare also enjoyed the game and has several references to bowls in his plays. In *The Taming of the Shrew*, Petruchio, satisfied that his taming of Kate is going well, remarks:

> *thus the bowl should run,*
> *And not unluckily against the bias.*

Retrace your steps over the A27, turn right to cross the Community Centre car park, and take the footpath

The Wriothesley Monument in the Southampton Chapel in St. Peter's Church, Titchfield. In the picture, Shakespeare's patron, the third Earl of Southampton, is shown as a small kneeling figure on the left-hand side of the tomb.

past the Community Association Youth Centre signed for the Village Centre. Cross the foot of Southampton Hill to walk down **Titchfield High Street.** Titchfield is as charming as its name. Streets of attractive houses—some half-timbered with jettied upper stories, others dating from the eighteenth century with rounded bow windows and pillared doorways—link arms around the marketplace overlooked by old coaching inns. On the right, **Barry's Cottages** were built by the Earl of Southampton's Trust in 1620. Shakespeare's patron, the third earl, took a keen interest in his estate and village, building an ironworks and reviving the woollen industry.

Turn left down Church Street to **St. Peter's Church.**
Dating from the late seventh or early eighth century, it is
one of Hampshire's finest churches. The porch is Anglo-
Saxon with a bonding course of reused Roman tiles. The
chapel at the south side of the chancel is dominated by the
massive, highly decorated Wriothesley monument erected
in 1594 by the third Earl of Southampton under the terms
of his father's will. Carved effigies commemorate the
second earl and his parents, the first earl and his countess.
The small figure of the third earl is shown kneeling at
prayer. No doubt the third earl was proud of his newly
erected monument, and Shakespeare probably had it in
mind when he wrote in a sonnet:

Not marble, nor the gilded monuments
Of princes, shall outlive this powerful rime.

Leave the church on your left, and walk beside a wall
on your right to cross a bridge over the **canal.** Once this
peaceful scene would have looked very different. In 1611
the third earl changed the world of Titchfield forever.
Before that date, the village was a thriving port at the head
of the large tidal estuary of the Meon, with wharves close
to the church busy with barges loading and unloading their
cargoes. The earl had a shingle bank built across the mouth
of the estuary with a sluice gate to regulate the flow of
water. This enlarged his estate with a freshwater haven but
put an end to Titchfield's trade. The navigable tidal
channel was replaced with a canal running from the village
to the coast, controlled by a sea lock. Horse-drawn barges
allowed the villagers to continue their trade, chiefly in
wool and hides. But this small-scale and slow method of
trading soon proved a failure.

Why should the earl have undertaken such an

ambitious project? Perhaps he intended to use his new water meadows—irrigated by channels bringing water from the canal—to produce early crops, or perhaps he really believed his canal would be successful. But as a keen sportsman, there is a possibility he was creating a splendid new area, rich in wildlife, where he and his friends could enjoy hunting, shooting and fishing. A map of his estate drawn in 1610 reveals his keen interest in hunting, with kennels for dogs clearly marked.

Although in his poems as well as his plays Shakespeare shows sympathy for hunted animals, there is no doubt he enjoyed the thrill of the chase and appreciated the finer points of a good hound. Perhaps the earl had a pack of hounds like those owned by Duke Theseus in *A Midsummer Night's Dream.* He tells his future bride, Hippolyta,

> My hounds are bred out of the Spartan kind,
> So flew'd, so sanded; and their heads are hung
> With ears that sweep away the morning dew.

The earl's reclaimed land is now the **Titchfield Haven Nature Reserve,** a rich and varied freshwater marsh which includes wet meadows, dense reedbeds, and lagoons that provide a paradise for birds. As it is so close to the sea, the Haven has become a refuge and feeding area for vast numbers of migrant birds, including Canada and Brent geese, in addition to nesting and resident species. Turn right to follow the path beside the canal that flows between masses of water-loving flowers such as marsh marigolds, purple loosestrife, and flowering rushes. On your left there are splendid views over the reserve. Cross a lane and continue straight ahead for about two miles through all gates, keeping to the towpath. You pass a bridge on the right marked with yellow arrow footpath signs, which is our return route. After another half-mile you will see the sea lock a few yards ahead. Pass a gate and a stile on your left, and keep ahead to read an interesting notice board giving details of the canal. Just to the left of the sea lock, before you reach the road, cross the stile on the left to join a woodland path. Turn right and follow the path as it eventually bears left to a gate opening to the road at the Meon shore.

Cross the road to enjoy the view over the Solent to the **Isle of Wight.** Then retrace your steps through the gate and along the path to the canal towpath. Turn right, with the canal now on your left, for about half a mile to the bridge marked by footpath signs. Turn left over the bridge and follow the field path, which shortly swings right to lead you over open fields. Thatched Little Posbrook Farm lies in a dip on your right. After passing a bungalow on your right, keep straight ahead beside a field towards the houses of Titchfield. Cross a farm track and continue along a narrow path that brings you to a meadow. Go over the meadow and past some garages. Continue along a path to the left of a high boarded fence, then keep ahead along the pavement to the foot of lower Belfield Road. Turn right down Coach Hill, then left along South Street to the High Street. Walk along the High Street and retrace your steps along the narrow footpath to return to your car in the Community Centre car park.

Walking with William Shakespeare

Starting point and parking

Titchfield is a large village between Southampton and Fareham, lying in the Meon valley just south of the A27. The walk starts from the Community Centre long stay car park. GR 541 061. Approaching from the west: Turn off the A27 following the sign "Titchfield village only." Drive down Southampton Hill past the short stay car park (parking there is limited to only three hours—this walk is too good to rush) and turn left (signed "Funtley") and follow the road around to the right. Turn left into Mill Street, marked with a no-through-road sign, then turn left into the Community Centre car park. Approaching from the east along the A27: Turn left following the Community Centre sign, then turn right into the car park.

Public transport

Titchfield is served by buses from Southampton and Portsmouth. For times, contact Traveline (0870) 608 2 608.

Length of walk: 5.5 miles.

Map: Ordnance Survey Explorer Map No 119.

Refreshments

Pubs and cafes in Titchfield. Coffee shop at the Abbey Garden Centre.

Place House is open April 1–September 30 daily, 10 AM to 6 PM; October 1–31 daily, 10 AM to 5 PM; November 1–March 31 daily, 10 AM to 4 PM. Admission free.

Titchfield Haven Nature Reserve can be visited by permit. Apply in advance to the Naturalist Warden, Haven Cottage, Cliff Road, Hill Head, Fareham, Hampshire; or telephone (01329) 662145.

THE WALK IN BRIEF

From the Community Centre car park entrance, turn left, cross the A27 via the pedestrian crossing, and walk down Mill Lane past the Garden Centre entrance to the entrance arch for Place House. Retrace your steps to the car park. Turn right across the car park and follow the sign for the Village Centre. Walk down High Street and turn left down Church Street. Leave the church on the left and walk with a wall on the right to cross the bridge over the canal. Turn right and follow the canal towpath (after 2 miles, note the bridge on the right with footpath signs— our return route). Pass a gate and a stile on the left, and cross a stile on the left by the sea lock just before the road. Bear right along the woodland path, which eventually curves left to a gate opening to the Meon shore. Retrace your steps along the canal towpath to the bridge (now on your left) with footpath signs. Turn left over the bridge and follow the field path ahead, which shortly curves right. Keep ahead towards Titchfield; cross a farm track to take a narrow hedged path to a meadow. Cross the meadow, pass garages on your left, and walk to the foot of Lower Belfield Road. Turn right down Coach Hill, then left along South Street to the High Street. Retrace your steps to the Community Centre car park.

CHAPTER 8

FORTUNES RESTORED:
IN LONDON WITH THE LORD CHAMBERLAIN'S MEN

The quality of mercy is not strain'd
It droppeth as the gentle rain from heaven
Upon the place beneath: it is twice blest,
It blesseth him that gives, and him that takes:
'Tis mightiest in the mightiest: it becomes
The throned monarch better than his crown.

—Portia, *The Merchant of Venice*

Portia's beautiful speech in praise of mercy must be one of the best-known passages in all Shakespeare's plays. When he wrote *The Merchant of Venice* in 1597, Shakespeare was at the height of his creative power. He could mold blank verse to suit every mood. He had made our native English language his own and forged new words when he needed them. And he had become an important member of a stable company of players—the Lord Chamberlain's Men. He was to stay with them for the rest of his career.

After the reopening of the playhouses in June 1594, Lord Strange's Men, led by James Burbage and his brilliant actor son, Richard, had formed a new company under the patronage of Lord Chamberlain Hunsdon. Shakespeare probably joined them shortly afterwards, as in March 1595 his name occurs along with those of William Kempe and Richard Burbage in a chamber account as payees for two performances at Greenwich Palace on December 26 and 27, 1594.

After acting with the Admiral's Company for ten days at Henslowe's playhouse at Newington Butts, the two companies separated. The Admiral's Men, with their star actor, Alleyn, went to another of Philip Henslowe's playhouses, the Rose in Southwark, where they continued to perform Christopher Marlowe's plays. The Lord Chamberlain's Men returned to the Theatre in Shoreditch with Shakespeare as their playwright and Richard Burbage as their leading actor. Their new patron, Lord Hunsdon, used his influence as the queen's cousin to prevail upon the mayor of the City of London to allow them to act plays in the Cross Keys Inn during the winter season.

In August 1596, when everything seemed to be going so well for him, Shakespeare suffered a heartbreaking loss. His only son, Hamnet, died at the age of eleven, a grief he was to mirror in *King John*. When Cardinal Pandulph accuses Constance of too much grief over the loss of her son, Arthur, she replies movingly, "He talks to me that never had a son." Perhaps he was able to attend the funeral with his family and was reminded that London was the place where he worked and lodged, but Stratford was home.

And Shakespeare was now in a position to restore the family fortunes. Twenty years previously, his father had applied for the status of a gentleman and failed. Now his son, wealthy and influential, was in a position to grant his father's wish. In October, only ten weeks after his son's death, Shakespeare went to the College of Arms in London and applied for a coat of arms and gentleman status for his father. He was successful. The motto on his coat of arms read, "Non Sanz Droict"—Not Without Right. In May 1597 Anne must have felt she had been rewarded for her patience when he bought one of the finest houses in Stratford: New Place.

At this time, a deeper note enters his plays as Shakespeare touches on themes that must have aroused strong feelings, even protests, among his audience. At a time when monarchs maintained their divine right to rule, it was risky to perform *Richard II*. Richard, who regards himself as "the deputy elected by the Lord," is forced to hand his crown to Bolingbroke. Then he is sent to Pomfret Castle and murdered. Shakespeare's own queen, Elizabeth, ruled without a husband but she had many suitors, one of whom was the Earl of Essex. Some of these suitors were of only political interest, but Essex had been a favorite all her life. Therefore, in 1601 when he led a rebellion against Elizabeth, we can imagine her fury. The evening before the rebellion, he paid the Lord Chamberlain's Men a large sum of money to put on a performance of *Richard II* in the hope it would incite the audience against the monarch. The planned coup never succeeded. Essex was imprisoned in the Tower of London for his folly, and retribution was wreaked on his followers. These included Shakespeare's patron, the Earl of Southampton, who was also sent to the Tower. The Lord Chamberlain's Men were now in an awkward position. One of the company, Augustine Phillips, managed to plead that money was their only incentive. However, the night before Essex's execution, Queen Elizabeth ordered them to perform *Richard II* before her at Whitehall Palace. Can we imagine the players' embarrassment? Perhaps this intelligent woman wanted to keep an eye on them, as she was heard to remark bitterly, "Know ye not I am Richard the Second?"

The Merchant of Venice, written only a year after the death of Hamnet, contains verse of great lyrical beauty, especially in the tender love scenes. The last act takes place at night in the garden of Portia's house at Belmont. Lorenzo speaks to Jessica as they await Portia's arrival:

> How sweet the moonlight sleeps upon this bank!
> Here will we sit, and let the sounds of music
> Creep in our ears: soft stillness and the night
> Become the touches of sweet harmony.

But running parallel with the love element in the play is another deep and highly controversial theme. The Jew, Shylock, tends to dominate the action as he demands a pound of flesh from Antonio, whose ships, in which his capital is invested, appear to have been lost. Unable to pay the money, Antonio awaits his fate in the courtroom as Shylock sharpens his knife. Like all Elizabethans at that time, Shakespeare had been brought up in a world that distrusted and disliked the Jewish people. Marlowe had scored a tremendous success with his play *The Jew of Malta*, in which the Jew, significantly named Barabbas, is an unmitigated villain. And anti-Jewish feeling was running high after the queen's physician, Lopez, a Portuguese Jew,

Middle Temple Hall, with its splendid double hammer beam roof and impressive carved screen, formed the setting for the first performance of Shakespeare's Twelfth Night *in February 1602*

had been accused of trying to poison her. But Shakespeare is not content to sacrifice his sympathy with the human predicament to satisfy public feeling. His Shylock is mean and vindictive but not wholly bad. Although he loves his money, he has also a genuine love for his daughter, Jessica. And he is allowed to state his case. Many times, he says, Antonio has mocked and scorned him because he is Jew. Shylock maintains Jews are human too: "Hath not a Jew eyes? Hath not a Jew hands . . . warm'd and cool'd by the same winter and summer as a Christian is? If you prick us do we not bleed, if you tickle us do we not laugh? If you poison us do we not die?" Remembering Lopez, there may have been a few murmurs among the crowd when they heard the last line!

Shakespeare was on safer ground in the two great history plays he wrote around this time, the first and second parts of *Henry IV*. In these plays we see the king growing weaker, facing rebellion among the northern earls and saddened by the wild behavior of his son, the Prince of Wales. The Elizabethans would have enjoyed the battle scenes culminating in the king's victory at Shrewsbury, but it was a comic figure that took audiences by storm. In Sir John Falstaff, the prince's boon companion, Shakespeare created one of the most famous characters in English literature. The Elizabethan audience loved him from the moment they saw his great round-bellied figure swagger

Blackfriars Lane and Playhouse Yard recall Shakespeare's London and Blackfriars Theatre, where his later plays were performed.

onto the stage. Here was a man happy to be himself. We might have expected better of a knight, but we find him drinking and whoring, cheating and lying, breaking all the laws of respectability. But he is no fool, and it is all done with the greatest good humor. As he spars with the prince in the Boar's Head tavern in Eastcheap and pretends to be dead on the battlefield at Shrewsbury, we laugh, but we also sympathize with him. After the battle, there was little hope for the wounded. If they lived, and were unable to support themselves, they were forced to beg. We feel there is some truth in his comments on honor: "Can honour set a leg? No. Or an arm? No. Or take away the grief of a wound? No." Like all great comic characters, his life is poised on the knife-edge of pathos. He pretends he is not old, fat, degenerate, a boaster and a coward, but he knows he is deluding himself. And we know too.

In *The Second Part of Henry IV*, the prince reforms and in a moving final scene is reconciled with his dying father. Falstaff, who has been busy in the Cotswolds persuading the foolish Justice Shallow to part with a thousand pounds, hears of his coronation and rushes to London to greet his former companion. I suspect when Henry spurns him with the words "I know thee not, old man: fall to thy prayers; / How ill white hairs become a fool and jester!" there were a few tears in the audience. Again, he deludes himself into thinking Henry would return to him, but he knows in his heart he will not.

Falstaff appears again in *The Merry Wives of Windsor*, but Shakespeare wrote this play in a hurry. (There is a tradition that he wrote the play at the request of the queen, who wanted to see the fat knight in love, and that she gave him only three weeks in which to write it.) It is almost all in prose and Falstaff is merely the butt of jokes, ending up being tipped in a ditch. But the real Falstaff is recalled in *Henry V* after his death in the Boar's Head tavern. His friends grieve for him, and the hostess describes his death in a marvellous speech that shows how well Shakespeare understood the thinking and language of ordinary folk. She is sure he is not in hell: "he's in Arthur's bosom. . . . A' made a finer end, and went away, an it had been any christom child. . . . after I saw him fumble with the sheets, and play with flowers, and smile upon his fingers' ends, I knew there was but one way; for his nose was as sharp as a pen, and a' babbled of green fields."

There is no doubt Shakespeare knew all there was to know about London taverns. He could have been living in one as he wrote the play (good food was available and could be eaten in private if wished, and candles were free). In 1596 Shakespeare had moved from St. Helen's in Bishopsgate and had crossed the river to the Liberty of the Clink in Southwark. Could he have taken a room at the

Elephant, recommended by Antonio to Sebastian in *Twelfth Night*? "In the south suburbs, at the Elephant, / Is best to lodge."

In the same year, the Lord Chamberlain's Men suffered a setback. The city corporation stopped all performances in the city inns, including the Cross Keys. Relations with their landlord, Giles Allen, at the Theatre were becoming increasingly acrimonious, and when the lease expired he threatened to pull the Theatre down. But James Burbage had made plans for a different sort of theater, one with a roof. He reckoned that the wealthier citizens of London would appreciate the warmth and comfort of an indoor auditorium and would be happy to pay a higher price for their tickets. This would compensate for the much smaller number it would be possible to accommodate. Much church property had come on the market after Henry VIII dissolved the monasteries, and Burbage was able to buy the Great Parliament Chamber, originally the upper frater of the former Dominican priory in the Liberty of Blackfriars. As a liberty, Blackfriars did not come under the jurisdiction of the City of London. He adapted the chamber as a theater, with a stage at one end and seating for all spectators. However, the rich inhabitants of Blackfriars objected and petitioned the Privy Council (the queen's closest advisors), and James was refused permission to use it. James died in 1597 and his son Richard surrendered the lease to Henry Evans and Nathaniel Giles for performances by one of the children's companies—the Children of the Chapel attached to St. Paul's—for performances presumably more suited to Blackfriars society.

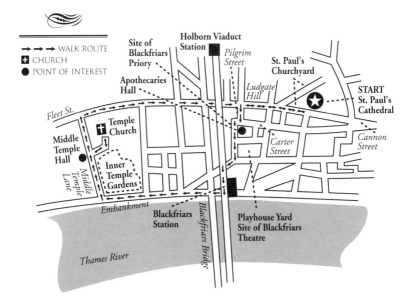

WALK ROUTE
CHURCH
POINT OF INTEREST

Site of Blackfriars Priory

Apothecaries Hall

Holborn Viaduct Station

Pilgrim Street

Ludgate Hill

St. Paul's Churchyard

START
St. Paul's Cathedral

Fleet St.

Temple Church

Middle Temple Hall

Inner Temple Gardens

Middle Temple Lane

Carter Street

Cannon Street

Embankment

Blackfriars Station

Blackfriars Bridge

Playhouse Yard
Site of Blackfriars Theatre

Thames River

H ow could the Lord Chamberlain's Men survive without a theater? Elizabethan players were resourceful and they found a brilliant answer, but that must wait until the next chapter! In this walk we remain north of the Thames. As the route is short, about two miles round, and also starts from St. Paul's Cathedral, it can be easily combined with the walk in chapter six. But this time we head west from the cathedral to visit the site of the Blackfriars Theatre and the magnificent Hall of the Middle Temple, one of the four Inns of Court that collectively in Elizabethan days formed what was virtually England's third university, devoted to the law. The great halls of the Inns of Court formed an ideal setting for masques and plays, which were immensely popular with all the members. On the evening of February 2, 1602, Shakespeare's *Twelfth Night* was performed for the first time in Middle Temple Hall.

The charming courtyard of the Apothecaries Hall in Blackfriars Lane

From the west entrance of **St. Paul's Cathedral,** walk past the statue of Queen Anne and continue down the southern side of Ludgate Hill, a wide, busy thoroughfare. Take the second turning on the left, **Pilgrim Street,** and enter a different world! Narrow lanes and courts with tunnel-like entrances twist south down to the river. In Shakespeare's time this was a superior theater district. Somewhere in this fascinating remnant of old London, the Bel Savage Inn once welcomed playgoers. They may have watched Shakespeare's early plays, as the inn's stage was used by the Queen's Men.

Pilgrim Street curves right to bring you to Ludgate Broadway—a deceptive name for an alley about 15 feet wide. On your left is **Carter Lane,** a charming alley opening to hidden courtyards well worth exploring if you have time. On the corner of Carter Lane, a plaque marks the site of the former Priory of Blackfriars. Shakespeare bought the gatehouse to the priory in 1613. Keep ahead down cobbled Blackfriars Lane. On your left you come to the impressive entrance to the **Apothecaries Hall** surmounted by the society's gilded crest. Through the entrance you come to a charming courtyard. The society can be traced back to the Guild of Pepperers formed in 1180 and has a royal charter dating from 1617. Past the hall entrance, the buildings give way to an open space on your left. This is still called **Playhouse Yard,** and you are now standing on the site of the former Blackfriars Theatre. In Shakespeare's time you would have seen a grand stone and timber building approached by a winding staircase. The theater was pulled down in August 1655 to make way for tenements, and *The Times* newspaper building now backs onto the deserted yard. But imagine the scene when Shakespeare's plays drew noisy colorful crowds jostling for admission! Shakespeare would have stood here, perhaps wondering how successful his latest play would be. With his keen business brain he was probably also assessing the size of the takings!

Continue down Blackfriars Lane and cross over Queen Victoria Street. Turn right to leave Blackfriars Station on your left, and shortly afterwards bear left to Blackfriars Bridge. Continue for a few yards along the bridge, then descend the steps on the left and turn right to follow the Embankment. Continue past Temple Avenue and the lawns of the **Inner Temple Gardens** to the tall iron gates at the entrance to cobbled Middle Temple Lane. Go through the gates to follow the gently sloping lane past the Temple Gardens. In these gardens the rival supporters of the houses of York and Lancaster began the Wars of the Roses, the Lancastrians choosing a red rose as their emblem, and the Yorkists a white one. In *The First Part of Henry VI*, Shakespeare depicts the scene in memorable verse. At the end, the Earl of Warwick comments:

> this brawl today,
> Grown to this faction in the Temple garden,

Shall send, between the red rose and the white,
A thousand souls to death and deadly night.

He was right: the wars were to last thirty-five years.

Follow the lane as it continues between the Middle Temple on the left and the Inner Temple on the right until you come on your left to **Fountain Court,** a small open space with a circular pool and single jet of water shaded by trees. **Middle Temple Hall** forms the south wall of the court, and the entrance to the hall is immediately on your left. The great hall of the Middle Temple is breathtaking. It is over a hundred feet long, the length of two tennis courts. It is spanned by a magnificent double hammer beam roof. The walls are panelled in the same dark oak and the splendid intricately carved oak screen is surmounted by a musicians' balcony. Begun in 1562 and finished in 1573, the hall has been at the center of student life for over four hundred years and is still so today. In 1602 Shakespeare's audience included the younger sons of the nobility and country gentry who wished to acquire some knowledge of the law, as well as those choosing law as their profession. Wealthy, intelligent, and high-spirited, they were among the first to appreciate Shakespeare as a poet, and they must have responded enthusiastically to the sparkling verse, the wit, and the fun of *Twelfth Night* when it was performed in their hall. Although today students follow law degrees at the universities, they must still dine "in hall" at certain times of the year, and when newly qualified, are first "called to the bar" in hall. The bar, known as the "cupboard," is a table made from the hatch covers of Sir Francis Drake's ship, *The Golden Hinde*.

After your visit to the hall, turn right from the entrance to go through a small arch signed for the Lamb Building. Walk through Elm Court past a delightful garden. Bear left up steps to the **Temple Church,** which

*The gardens of the Inner Temple, still colorful with white and red roses—
symbols of the Wars of the Roses*

Shakespeare must have known well. The building has a
distinctive appearance. The long chancel is known as the
"Oblong," and the circular nave is known as the "Round."
The round church was built first and consecrated in 1185
as a chapel to serve the London headquarters of the
Knights Templar, a military order of knights founded to
protect pilgrims traveling to the Holy Land. So the area
became known as "the Temple," the name it still bears
today. The Oblong was built later, after King Henry III had
expressed a wish to be buried in the church. To provide a
suitable setting for his tomb, a new chancel was built and
consecrated in 1240. However, the king changed his mind
and was buried in Westminster Abbey. After the
suppression of the Order of the Knights Templar in 1307,

the Temple was eventually rented to two colleges of lawyers, who formed separate establishments known as the Inner and Middle Temples. In 1608 King James granted them ownership of the land, provided they maintained the church.

Inside this beautiful church there is much to admire. Clusters of slim grey-green Purbeck marble columns soar to a simply vaulted roof. The great east window is a lovely example of modern stained glass. Glowing with rich color, it was a gift from the Glaziers' Company in 1954 to replace windows destroyed during the Second World War. In the Round you will find effigies of the Knights Templar dating from the twelfth and thirteenth centuries. They lie cross-legged in armor on the paving beneath which they were buried. Though battered by time, they retain a stern dignity.

Leave the church and turn right to walk through the arcade to return to Middle Temple Lane. Turn right up the lane and leave the peace of the Temple precincts and emerge in the bustle of Fleet Street. Turn right again up Fleet Street, across Ludgate Circus and up Ludgate Hill to return to our starting point, St. Paul's Cathedral.

Elm Court, opposite the Lamb Building in the Temple grounds

Starting point: St. Paul's Cathedral.

Nearest tube station: St. Paul's.

Length of walk: 2 miles.

Map
Supplement my directions with a good London map.

NB: Make sure you do this walk on a weekday, as the Temple is closed at weekends. Middle Temple Hall is open for visitors Monday through Friday, 10 AM to noon, and 3 PM to 4 PM. Telephone: (020) 7427 4820/4800.

The entrance to the courtyard of the Apothecaries Hall is open on weekdays. The hall can be visited by prior appointment with the beadle. Telephone: (020) 7236 1189.

THE WALK
IN BRIEF

Head west from St. Paul's Cathedral down Ludgate Hill. Turn left along Pilgrim Street, which curves right to Ludgate Broadway. The site of Blackfriars Priory is opposite you. Leave Carter Street on your left and continue down cobbled Blackfriars Lane past the Apothecaries Hall to Playhouse Yard, the site of the Blackfriars Theatre. Keep ahead to cross the road in front of Blackfriars Station. Turn right, then bear left onto Blackfriars Bridge. Continue for a few yards along the bridge, then descend the steps on the left to the Embankment. Turn right along the Embankment past the Inner Temple Gardens to the iron gates at the entrance to Middle Temple Lane. Turn right through the gates and follow the lane to the Middle Temple Hall at the southern side of Fountain Court. Leave the hall and turn right through an arch signed for the Lamb Building. Keep ahead through Elm Court, go up the steps and bear left to see the Temple Church. Leave the church, turn right through the arcade to rejoin Middle Temple Lane. Turn right to walk up the lane and go through the gate into Fleet Street. Turn right to walk up Fleet Street and Ludgate Hill to return to St. Paul's Cathedral.

CHAPTER 9

A MUSE OF FIRE:
"THE GREAT GLOBE ITSELF"

> But pardon, gentles all,
> The flat unraised spirits that have dared
> On this unworthy scaffold to bring forth
> So great an object; can this cockpit hold
> The vasty fields of France? Or may we cram
> Within this wooden O the very casques
> That did affright the air at Agincourt?
> —Prologue to the first act of *Henry V*

W ith the Theatre under threat from the landlord and their newly acquired Blackfriars building unusable, the Lord Chamberlain's Men were in a desperate position. But although the leader of the company, James Burbage, was dead, his enterprising spirit lived on in his sons! Richard and his brother, Cuthbert, secured a thirty-one-year lease on a plot of land in Southwark, not far from the Rose in Maiden Lane. In December 1598, or January the following year, the brothers, accompanied by their carpenter, Peter Street, and "divers other persons to the number of twelve," dismantled the Theatre—they had the right to the building—and carried the pieces over the frozen river to Southwark. By autumn, the most famous of Elizabethan playhouses, the Globe, was finished and ready for them.

Unlike Philip Henslowe, who took complete charge of the Admiral's Company, hiring and paying his actors himself, the Lord Chamberlain's Men, in order to finance the building of the Globe, formed a joint stock company, the shares in which were saleable. The Burbage brothers owned fifty percent of the shares; Shakespeare, Augustine Phillips, Thomas Pope, John Heminge, and William Kempe each had ten percent. Shakespeare was also one of the "housekeepers" responsible for the payment of ground-rent and the upkeep of the theater. At the end of a performance, the "gatherers" who had collected the entrance money for the galleries and the yard, would produce their boxes. The actor-sharers would give half the gallery takings to the housekeepers (as both a sharer and a housekeeper, Shakespeare would do well), pay the hired men, and keep the rest. Shakespeare, as chief playwright, actor, sharer and housekeeper, was more deeply involved in the life of the theater than anyone else. And he was now financially secure.

The Lord Chamberlain's Men performed their first play

The present-day Globe Theatre stands on the south bank of the Thames, only a short distance from the site of the original Globe

at the Globe in the autumn of 1599, and Shakespeare had a new play for them: *Henry V*. It was a play that they must have known could not fail to appeal to the patriotic Elizabethan audience keen to cheer an English victory, particularly if won against the odds. It is possible that the opening play was *Julius Caesar*, which a foreign visitor records seeing performed at the Globe on September 21, 1599, but I feel that it is more likely they would open with a play with an English theme. The reference to Essex in the Prologue to Act V suggests that Shakespeare wrote *Henry V* between Essex's departure for Ireland on March 27, 1599, and his return on September 28. Shakespeare confidently predicts that Essex will return, "bringing rebellion broached on his sword." If he had written the play any later, he would have known that Essex returned in disgrace.

Henry V is the most patriotic of Shakespeare's history plays. However doubtful Henry's claims to the French throne may be (and Shakespeare makes a brave and rather long-winded effort to justify them), the magnificent verse, as Henry leads his ragged army to face the French at Agincourt, has echoed down the centuries. It was still capable of rallying the nation in the twentieth century. When Winston Churchill praised the handful of pilots who won the Battle of Britain during the Second World War with the words, "never in the field of human conflict was so much owed by so many to so few," he recalled Henry addressing his troops before Agincourt: "We few, we happy few, we band of brothers."

Shakespeare makes it very clear which side he is on. Henry and the English nobles are firm, upright characters, unwavering as they face the foppish and overconfident French. The difference between the two armies is stressed to win our sympathy. The English army, though tired and weakened by illness, is resolute and determined. The odds against an English victory are five to one. But again Shakespeare raises deeper issues as he explores the nature of kingship. On the eve of the battle, Henry talks to a group of soldiers around their campfire. They make the point that if the war is unjust and they die in support of their king, they have little hope of salvation. Henry argues that it would not be so, but their view worries him:

> Upon the king!—let us our lives, our souls,
> Our debts, our careful wives,
> Our children, and our sins, lay on the king!
> We must bear all.

It is a tribute to Shakespeare's amazing versatility that as the century turned and he was writing one of his greatest tragedies, *Hamlet,* he also wrote a sparkling comedy, *Twelfth*

Night. The play opens and concludes with music and contains some of Shakespeare's loveliest songs. Orsino, the Duke of Illyria, is trying without success to woo Olivia, a rich young widow who is mourning the recent death of her brother. Viola and her twin brother, Sebastian, are shipwrecked separately on the Illyrian coast and each fears the other is dead. Viola disguises herself as a boy, Cesario—a frequent device in Shakespeare's plays, written when boy actors had to play the parts of girls. In her disguise as Cesario, she becomes a favorite with Orsino and is sent by him to plead on his behalf with Olivia. Unfortunately Olivia falls in love with the disguised Viola and she falls in love with the duke! All is put right with the appearance of Sebastian.

Woven into these romantic tangles is an amusing subplot. The peace of Olivia's household is shattered by the nightly carousing of her uncle, Sir Toby Belch, and his foolish friend, Sir Andrew Aguecheek. Olivia's steward, Malvolio, offends them with his Puritanical officiousness and vanity. They get their revenge when Maria, Olivia's maid, fools Malvolio into thinking Olivia really does love him. He appears all smiles before her, cross-gartered and in yellow stockings. Pretending he is mad, the conspirators have him taken away and confined in a dark room. There he is teased unmercifully, and although the Elizabethan playgoers would be pleased to see a Puritan suffer—if the high-minded Puritans had succeeded in getting their way there would have been no theaters—a modern audience may feel the joke has gone too far. But Shakespeare is fair to Malvolio. He is shown as a trusted servant, valued by Olivia; in trying to ensure peaceful nights he is only doing his duty, however irritating he is in the process. *Twelfth Night* has everything: a cleverly contrived plot, lyrical verse, and a great deal of fun.

But these were difficult times. The optimism of the

The splendid stage in the Globe Theatre

early years of Elizabeth's reign was giving way to disillusionment. The aged queen would not name her successor, and bad harvests led to unrest throughout the country. "The rain it raineth every day," sings the Clown at the end of *Twelfth Night*. It is estimated that half the population of Stratford were paupers. The Earl of Southampton, whose friendship Shakespeare must have still valued, had supported his hero, the Earl of Essex, in his abortive rebellion, and in February 1601 Southampton was convicted of treason and sentenced to death. His mother's pleading saved his life, but he was sent to the Tower. (While a prisoner, he had his portrait painted with his favorite cat, who scaled the walls to be with him!)

On September 8, Shakespeare suffered a private grief when he attended the burial of his father. The time was indeed "out of joint." Shakespeare, who saw life in all its aspects, had still to explore the darker side of human existence, to confront the tremendous problem that all must face at some time: how to cope with evil. Unlike the heroes in Greek tragedy whose fate is ruled by destiny,

Walking with William Shakespeare

Shakespeare's tragic heroes are real people who fail because they cannot overcome a potentially disastrous fault in themselves.

Hamlet is the story of a fundamentally good, highly intelligent man, "th'expectancy and rose of the fair state, / The glass of fashion and the mould of form," suddenly confronted by the ghost of his murdered father and commanded to avenge his death. There are no practical difficulties in Hamlet's way. The murderer, his uncle Claudio, is close at hand. Claudio is now king and holding court at Elsinore with Queen Gertrude, Hamlet's mother, whom he married soon after the killing. Hamlet cannot bring himself to do the deed. He thinks about it, makes plans, deludes himself into thinking he needs more proof, contemplates committing suicide, and plays for time by pretending to be mad. He sees his mother's hasty marriage to her former husband's brother as incest (which by Elizabethan standards it was) and in a fury against all women spurns Ophelia, whom he loves: "Get thee to a nunnery; why wouldst thou be a breeder of sinners?" If he acts on impulse, he can be decisive—he kills Polonius, who is eavesdropping behind a curtain—but given time to think, he can do nothing. He recognizes this characteristic in himself as he voices his thoughts aloud to the audience, in one of his famous soliloquies:

> And thus the native hue of resolution
> Is sicklied o'er with the pale cast of thought,
> And enterprises of great pith and moment,
> With this regard their currents turn awry,
> And lose the name of action....

How effective the soliloquy must have been in such an intimate theater with many of the audience within touching distance! And even in this profound and soul-searching play, Shakespeare remains an actor. A group of players visit Elsinore, and Hamlet (one would imagine he would have other matters on his mind) tells them how they must deliver their speeches: "Speak the speech, I pray you, as I pronounced it to you, trippingly on the tongue; but if you mouth it, as many of your players do, I had as lief the town-crier spoke my lines." *Hamlet* was, and has remained, one of Shakespeare's most successful plays.

In 1602 Shakespeare moved back across the Thames to lodge with a French Huguenot family, the Mountjoys. Their house lay just within the northwest corner of the city walls, on the corner of Silver Street and Muggle Street. They made the splendid jewelled headdresses, known as tires, worn by the court ladies. One of their clients was Anne of Denmark, wife of James I. Through them Shakespeare would hear all the court gossip as nobles jostled for power around a queen who, with only a short time to live, still refused to name her successor. No one could predict the future: some hoped for better times; some feared the worst. In this atmosphere, Shakespeare's mood darkened further as he explored the fatal effect of jealousy on an otherwise noble mind in *Othello*.

Othello is a brave Moor who has secretly married Desdemona, the beautiful daughter of a Venetian senator. He is black, and Shakespeare is not afraid to set this play against a background of racism as well as jealousy. For Desdemona's father, Brabantio, the marriage of his daughter to Othello, noble though he is, must have been brought about by "foul charms." Othello answers him simply:

> She loved me for the dangers I had past;
> And I loved her that she did pity them.

Desdemona declares her love for her husband, and the duke gives his blessing, saying to Brabantio:

If virtue no delighted beauty lack
Your son-in-law is far more fair than black.

Othello's ensign, Iago, is jealous of the Moor's successes and angry because he has not been promoted. While pretending to be Othello's friend, he convinces him by subtle suggestion and trickery that Desdemona is unfaithful. Unable to control his jealousy, "eaten up with passion," Othello insults her and, deciding she must die, comes to her room at night. As his love and jealousy war with one another, he kisses her. She awakes, and in a highly charged emotional scene he strangles her. Othello, when finally convinced of her innocence, describes himself as "one that loved not wisely, but too well." Life has nothing to offer him now, and he kills himself, falling on Desdemona's body. The dramatic intensity of this scene and the magnificent quality of the verse moved contemporary audiences to tears.

In March 1603 Queen Elizabeth died, naming as her successor King James VI of Scotland, the son of Mary Queen of Scots. He would be James I of England. He was awkward and pedantic, but he was also intelligent, with a keen interest in literature. He had already expressed his views on poetry in his *Essays of a Prentice in the Divine Art of Poetry* and *Poetical Exercises at Vacant Hours*. Both James and his wife, Anne, loved plays. By letters patent on May 19, as he was making his stately progress south from Scotland, James lost no time in making the Lord Chamberlain's Men part of the royal household. As his servants and grooms of the chamber, the King's Men, as they were now called, were authorized "to use and exercise the Arte and faculty of playinge" throughout the kingdom. But temporarily, at least, there was no possibility of performing in London. The arrival of James in the city coincided with a severe outbreak of the plague. The coronation had to be delayed. James toured the southern counties and the theaters were closed. The court spent the winter months at Hampton Court, and between December 1603 and February 1604 the King's Men entertained the royal household with eight plays, more than twice as many as the average during Elizabeth's reign. For the coronation the following March, the King's Men were in attendance, resplendent in scarlet robes.

The theaters reopened in 1605. The King's Men were fully occupied with performances at the Globe and at court, touring the major towns during the summer. Shakespeare was seeing and experiencing more of life at court, and he must have compared the needless extravagance he witnessed with the poverty and suffering he saw daily in the countryside and the teeming city streets. This contrast must have dominated his mind as, in his room in Silver Street or in one of the neighboring inns, he wrote that great outcry against cruelty in all its forms: *King Lear*. With his characteristic sympathy, he piles horror on horror, demanding our pity for all who suffer, whether they be king or pauper.

Like all Shakespeare's tragic heroes, Lear, King of Britain, is partly responsible for his own fate, being foolishly susceptible to flattery. Now over eighty, he decides to retire and divide the kingdom among his three daughters. The larger shares will be given to the ones who say they love him most. The two wicked sisters, Goneril and Regan, flatter him with fulsome protestations of love; the youngest, Cordelia, although she loves her father, recognizes the folly of the proceedings and refuses to join the flatterers. Spurned by her father, Cordelia leaves Britain to marry the King of France. Lear is sure Goneril and Regan will welcome him, but now they show their true colors and cruelly refuse him shelter, turning him out into a violent storm with his faithful Fool. In a harrowing scene, he defies the storm and now, stripped of power, without a roof over his head, he is forced to face the truth. He recognizes his folly in trusting flatterers and realises that lives, like his own, are destroyed by evil, deceit and cruelty. Through his own suffering, he is brought to feel for others:

> Poor naked wretches, whereso'er you are,
> That bide the pelting of this pitiless storm,
> How shall your houseless heads and unfed sides,
> Your loopt and window'd raggedness, defend you
> From seasons such as this! O! I have ta'en
> Too little care of this. Take physic, pomp;
> Expose thyself to feel what wretches feel.

There are moments of calm in the play when Cordelia's gentle kindness restores Lear's sanity after his sufferings have driven him mad, and we hope all may be well. But Shakespeare does not allow us to relax. At the end of the play the wicked characters are all dead, but not before the captive Lear enters with Cordelia dead in his arms. Heartbroken, the old king mourns:

> No, no, no life!
> Why should a dog, a horse, a rat have life,
> And thou no breath at all? . . .

Shakespeare has wrung our hearts but all is not lost. There is always hope. Before he also dies, Lear looks at Cordelia:

> Do you see this? Look on her, look, her lips,
> Look there, look there!

Does he die happy, thinking she is still alive? And there is a final note of acceptance as the king's faithful friend, the Earl of Kent, says:

Vex not his ghost: O, let him pass! He hates him
That would upon the rack of this tough world
Stretch him out longer.

There could be no greater protest against what
Wordsworth called "man's inhumanity to man" than
Shakespeare's *King Lear*. It was a strange choice for a
Christmas entertainment, but it was performed before King
James at Whitehall "upon Saint Stephen's night" 1606. But
the king was in somber mood. On November 5th the
previous year, an attempt had been made to kill him along
with his family and all the Lords and Commons assembled
in Parliament. The Gunpowder Plot, as this assassination
attempt came to be called, failed. Today in England
everyone celebrates the failure with fireworks and bonfires
on which effigies of the ringleader, Guy Fawkes, are
burned. But at the time, the Gunpowder Plot shocked the
nation. There was a spontaneous feeling of sympathy
towards the king, not always a favorite on account of his
Scottish upbringing. Shakespeare, always sensitive to the
mood of his audience, was prompted to write a Scottish
play, *Macbeth*.

The whole action of *Macbeth* takes place in an
atmosphere of fear and tension. The emphasis is on
darkness and night, with all its attendant horrors. Again we
have a tragic hero with noble qualities. When we first meet
him, Macbeth appears as a brave soldier and a good friend,
eager, after fighting in support of his king, Duncan, to
return to his home and the wife he loves. His fault, as he
openly confesses, is "vaulting ambition, which o'erleaps
itself / And falls on th'other." When tempted by evil, he is
unable to resist. The play opens with a storm, a suitable
accompaniment for three weird sisters cackling ominously
as they plan to meet Macbeth. They meet him and his
friend, Banquo, and prophesy that soon Macbeth will be

honored with another title, thane of Cawdor, and that in the future he will be king. He starts—the idea was already in his mind. But to his alarm, they also prophesy that Banquo's children shall be kings. (King James would have been pleased: he believed he was descended from a lord who was called Banquo, and Shakespeare cleverly portrayed this character as noble and incorruptible throughout the play.) Macbeth sends a messenger with a letter to inform Lady Macbeth of the prophecies. She decides immediately to help her husband fulfill the prophecy, calls his reluctance cowardice, and, when Duncan arrives at their castle to spend the night, persuades Macbeth to murder him. Her hands become red with Duncan's blood as she smears the faces and hands of the sleeping guards. Duncan's son, Malcolm, escapes to England. Macbeth is now "steep'd in blood" and, realizing that the prophecy about Banquo may also prove true, he hires murderers to kill him and his son, Fleance. Banquo dies but Fleance escapes. Scotland is suffering under Macbeth's kingship and some Scottish nobles are growing suspicious. One of them, Macduff, leaves his family behind and joins Malcolm. Furious, Macbeth orders all in Macduff's castle to be slain, including his wife and children. He visits the witches again and is reassured when they tell him he will be safe until Birnam Wood comes to Dunsinane, and that "none of woman born shall harm Macbeth."

Malcolm and Macduff, at the head of an army, march towards Dunsinane. To conceal their numbers, they cut branches from Birnam Wood. Macbeth, standing on the battlements, sees to his horror that the witch's prophecy is coming true—Birnam Wood is coming to Dunsinane. At this moment he is told that his wife is dead. He has loved her and is weary of the world:

> Life's but a walking shadow, a poor player
> That struts and frets his hour upon the stage
> And then is heard no more: it is a tale
> Told by an idiot, full of sound and fury,
> Signifying nothing.

But his courage does not weaken. He goes out to fight, and the final prophecy is fulfilled when he is killed by Macduff, who tells him he was "from his mother's womb / Untimely ript." The play ends with Malcolm inviting everyone to Scone to witness his coronation.

The play can be interpreted in a metaphysical light. The witches could be seen as personifications of Macbeth's own evil inclinations, offering what appear to be chances of future happiness but leading finally to his downfall. The ghostly apparitions in the play could be seen as products of Macbeth's own fevered imagination. But to Shakespeare's audience, the witches and apparitions were real. James was highly superstitious and took a personal interest in witches. In 1597 he had written a book about Scottish witches, *Demonology*, which Shakespeare read. The play would have fascinated James and was probably performed at court (along with *King Lear*) in 1606. With fine verse to please the more discerning, and witches, ghosts, and strange apparitions to hold the groundlings spellbound, Shakespeare had no difficulty in satisfying his wider audience in the Globe.

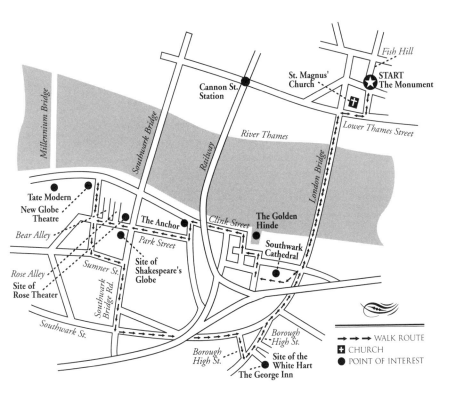

The highlight of this walk south of the Thames is a tour of the new Globe Theatre built only a short distance from the site of the original Globe on Bankside in Southwark. The whole area is rich in reminders of the great poet. Our starting point is the **Monument**, built to commemorate the Great Fire of 1666, which burned for five days and devastated the city. It stands at the foot of Fish Street, close to the north end of London Bridge. Shakespeare knew this part of London well: "Up Fish Street! Down Saint Magnus' corner! Kill and knock down! Throw them into Thames!" cries the rebel leader Jack Cade as he leads his followers from Southwark across London Bridge in *The Second Part of Henry VI*. Leave the Monument on your left and walk downhill to St. Magnus' Church in Lower Thames Street.

Southwark Cathedral, at one time Shakespeare's parish church

Cross the road and turn right, with the church on your left. After about 50 yards, take the pedestrian subway signed for London Bridge. Bear right, following the sign for London Bridge West Side and Southwark Cathedral. Go up the steps to cross **London Bridge.**

As you cross, you have a splendid view of the river on both sides, but Shakespeare, on his way over the London Bridge of his day (built in 1209), would have seen very little of the water. It was a narrow, crowded thoroughfare lined with houses several stories high. The road between the houses was barely nine feet wide in places. Pedestrians must have endured many hazardous journeys dodging horses and carriers' carts! But if they were in search of entertainment they would feel the risks were well worth taking, for Southwark, a liberty outside the City's jurisdiction, offered all they needed: taverns, gaming houses, brothels, the bull- and bear-baiting ring, and, more recently, the playhouses. When the Globe opened in 1599, there were already three playhouses in Southwark: the Swan, the Hope and the Rose. But the Globe, with

Walking with William Shakespeare

Shakespeare as its playwright and an excellent company of actors including the brilliant Richard Burbage, soon attracted the largest crowds. Sometimes over three thousand spectators crammed the yard and galleries. Shakespeare had moved across the river in 1596 and taken lodgings on Bankside, possibly at an inn. After the Globe was finished, he moved to a small house adjoining the theater. His parish church was St. Saviour's, now **Southwark Cathedral**.

Turn right, and descend the steps to the left of the cathedral, and continue to the main entrance. This fine Gothic church has dominated the south bank of the river for over nine hundred years. Originally it was part of an Augustinian monastery, but after Henry VIII dissolved the religious houses, the people of Southwark claimed it as their parish church. It is a beautiful building with many treasures, but it has a special quality. Perhaps the appeal of this unassuming church is best summed up by the Dean in his foreword to the guidebook: "This is not a Cathedral of mighty abbots, kings and politicians, it is a Cathedral of mostly ordinary people who found their lives changed by faith such that they achieved much more than they ever imagined possible."

For Shakespeare, St. Saviour's held a sad memory. His brother Edmund, sixteen years his junior, had followed him to London hoping to make his name as an actor. He died in December 1607, aged twenty-seven, and Shakespeare arranged for his burial in the church—a mark of respect seldom paid to an actor. The sexton's note reads: "Edmund Shakespeare, a player, buried in the church with a forenoone knell of the great bell, twenty shillings." The fee for burial in the churchyard was only two shillings and that for ringing the lesser bell only one shilling, so the funeral was expensive. Most funerals took place in the afternoon, and holding it in the morning added to the expense.

Probably Shakespeare arranged a morning funeral for his brother to allow his fellow actors to be present, as theater performances began at two o'clock. **Edmund's commemorative stone** is in the chancel. His name is spelled "Edmond."

Shakespeare's own **memorial** is situated at the east end of the south aisle. It depicts Shakespeare reclining rather uncomfortably in a Bankside meadow with St. Saviour's Church, Winchester Palace (Southwark was in the diocese of Winchester), and the Globe and Rose theaters in the background. Above the memorial is a colorful window filled with characters from his plays. On the right of the memorial is a tablet commemorating the American actor Sam Wanamaker, who inspired the building of the present day Globe Theatre.

A door from the north choir aisle leads into the Harvard Chapel, and here we discover a series of interesting links with Shakespeare, Stratford and America. John Harvard, the major benefactor of the famous New England university, was born in Southwark in 1607. His mother, Katherine, had lived in Stratford before her marriage. (See chapter 3.) It is quite likely that Shakespeare knew her and also knew John's father, Robert, a prominent townsman and one of St. Saviour's churchwardens. The east window is by an American artist, John La Farge, and includes the arms of Harvard University and Emmanuel College, Cambridge, where John read for his degree.

Leave the cathedral by the main entrance and turn right through the garden. Turn right again along Cathedral Street to see the superb replica of *The Golden Hinde,* the ship in which Sir Francis Drake circumnavigated the world in 1580. Bear right, past the ship, then turn left by Pickford's Wharf. You are now walking down Clink Street, named after one of Southwark's prisons, which we shall shortly see. The ruins on your left are all that remain of the

The Shakespeare memorial in Southwark Cathedral. Characters from his plays are depicted in the window above, with Prospero from The Tempest *a commanding figure in the center. The plaque on the right of the memorial pays tribute to Sam Wanamaker, who inspired the building of the present-day Globe Theatre.*

Bishop of Winchester's Palace, which was in use until the end of the seventeenth century. The house once had a large garden where the bishop could wander among his flowers and fruit trees while prisoners sat miserably in their damp cells close by. You come to the entrance to the **Clink Prison Museum** on your left. From the grim gateway, steps lead down into what appears to be a dark tunnel. If you have the nerve, you can descend the steps and, as the notice board states, "do your stretch in the Clink"! It is a relief to leave this gloomy alley and emerge opposite the Anchor Inn. Turn left and after a few yards turn right into Park Street. In Shakespeare's day this was called Maiden Lane and would have been thronged with eager crowds of playgoers, as his company's Globe stood on one side of the road and Henslowe's Rose a few yards away on the other side.

Continue over Porter Street to the **site of the original Globe** on your left. A large bronze plaque bears Shakespeare's portrait with London Bridge and Bankside in the background. A small area of the foundations was

The simple lime-washed exterior of the Globe. The gates close to the perimeter wall are decorated with small animals, birds, insects and plants illustrating quotations from Shakespeare.

uncovered in 1989, and it was possible to evaluate though not excavate them. However, they provided valuable information. Cross the road, and shortly you come to Rose Alley on your right with a large office block on the corner. The foundations of the **Rose Theatre** lie under the office block and parts of them have been excavated. Guided tours of the site are arranged by the Globe management when it is not possible to tour the theater.

Pass **Bear Gardens,** a reminder that the bear-baiting arena, with all its horrors, provided an alternative to the nearby playhouses for the Elizabethans. Turn right along New Globe Walk, which brings you to the entrance to the new **Globe Theatre.** Built, as far as was possible, to the same specifications, with the same materials, and using the same methods as the original Globe, this splendid theater is, to quote the guidebook, "the work of many people and the dream of one man," Sam Wanamaker, CBE. Convinced Shakespeare deserved more than a bronze plaque, Sam Wanamaker was the driving force behind a worldwide effort to do our greatest poet justice.

As soon as you enter the building, you are absorbed into Shakespeare's world. You can enjoy an excellent guided tour that lasts up to an hour and browse through a fascinating exhibition revealing many of the Elizabethan actors' secrets. For instance, you can discover how they managed to fly across the stage and produce convincing sound effects.

The theater is carefully modelled on the circular Elizabethan plan. For Ben Jonson, the first Globe was the "glory of the Banke" [Bankside], and I see no reason why he should not say the same today! Outside, the theater is lime-washed, but inside, like the original Globe, it is brilliantly colorful. The Elizabethans saw the theater as an image of an ordered universe. The rectangular stage projecting halfway into the yard, where each man played his part, was earth. Beneath the stage lay hell, accessed by a trapdoor, and the richly decorated canopy above the stage, accessed by a smaller trapdoor, was the "heavens." Spectators standing in the yard or sitting in the three tiers of galleries surrounding the stage were enclosed in their own small world. The new Globe, following the same pattern, gives the same impression. There is no barrier between actors and audience and, as in Elizabethan times, there are matinee (daylight) performances. The stage is not lit for evening performances and the theater lighting simulates daylight. Actors and audience can see each other and everyone shares the same interactive experience. Shakespeare may have written for a sixteenth-century audience, but this is a surprisingly modern concept!

To continue the walk, leave the Globe Theatre by the

main entrance to return to New Globe Walk. Turn right and keep ahead across Park Street to the junction with Sumner Street. Turn left along Sumner Street to Southwark Bridge Road. Cross the road and turn right. Keep ahead past Thrale Street on the left until you come to Southwark Street just before a railway bridge. Cross the road and turn left. Follow Southwark Street as it runs under a railway bridge and take the next turning on the right, signed "Borough High Street." This appears odd, as it is heading south, but I do have a reason for the diversion, as you will discover! This short street leads to a war memorial. Bear left to cross the road—the Borough High Street proper—and turn left to head north. After a few yards you come to the entrance way to the **George Inn.** Now the property of the National Trust, this former coaching inn is the last galleried inn left in London. The yard is still there, with heavily balustraded galleries linking the bedrooms on the first and second floors. The present inn was built in 1677 on the site of a much older building that surrounded the yard where plays were performed. Shakespeare may have known the George—perhaps even acted there. A little further along the High Street you come to **White Hart Yard,** the site of an inn he immortalized in *The Second Part of Henry VI.* We meet Jack Cade again, appealing to his followers to stay with him, crying, "Hath my sword therefore broke through London gates, that you should leave me at the White Hart in Southwark?"

Pass Southwark Cathedral on your left and retrace your steps over London Bridge to return to our starting point near the Monument.

The nave of Southwark Cathedral

Starting point
The Monument near the north end of London Bridge.

Nearest tube station
Monument.

Length of walk
2 miles.

Map
Supplement my sketch map with a good London map.

For information about the Shakespeare's Globe Exhibition, Globe Theatre tours, and times of performances, see the website *www.shakespeares-globe.org,* or telephone (020) 7902 1500 (enquiries) or (020) 7401 9919 (box office). There is a shop, café and restaurant open daily.

Southwark Cathedral offers audio tour wands to enable you to explore its rich history, or you can book a guided tour through the Visitors' Officer. Telephone (020) 7367 6734 or visit the website *www.southwark.anglican.org/cathedral.* The cathedral has a shop and restaurant.

The Clink Prison Museum is open 10 AM to 6 PM every day (8 PM Saturday and Sunday). Telephone: (020) 7403 6515.

L eave the Monument on your left and descend the hill to Lower Thames Street. Turn right, leaving St. Magnus' Church on your left, and take the pedestrian subway to London Bridge West Side. Cross the bridge to Southwark Cathedral. Turn right and descend the steps to the left of the cathedral to reach the main entrance. After your visit, turn right from the cathedral main entrance, then right again along Cathedral Street to see *The Golden Hinde*. Bear left at Pickford's Wharf along Clink Street to emerge opposite the Anchor Inn. Turn left for a few yards, then right into Park Street to pass the site of the original Globe theater on your left and Rose Alley on your right. Turn right along New Globe Walk to the new Globe Theatre. After your visit, turn right from the entrance along New Globe Walk to Sumner Street. Turn left along Sumner Street to Southwark Bridge Road. Cross the road and turn right. Just before a railway bridge, turn left along Southwark Street. After going under a railway bridge take the next road on the right (heading south), signed "Borough High Street." At the war memorial, cross the road on your left, Borough High Street proper, and turn left (heading north). After a few yards, look for the entrance to the George Inn and, a little farther on, White Hart Yard. Continue over London Bridge, retracing your steps to the Monument.

CHAPTER 10

CHANGING TIMES:
HOME IN STRATFORD

There's beggary in the love that can be reckoned.
—Mark Antony, *Antony and Cleopatra*

By the summer of 1607, Shakespeare had written his great celebration of mature love, *Antony and Cleopatra*. Although the play followed closely on *Macbeth* and could be said to be a tragedy, it is entirely different in tone. There is no sense of the agonizing inward struggles, self-delusion, and deceit that we find in the other tragedies. The witch-haunted mists of Scotland give way to the warming rays of the Egyptian sun, the dark corridors of chilly castles to the soft beds of the East. Shakespeare takes his story from Sir Thomas North's translation of Plutarch's *Lives* and enriches it with his finest poetry.

Mark Antony, Octavius Caesar, and Lepidus are triumvirs of Rome, sharing control over the vast Roman Empire. Enemies, including Pompey with his strong fleet, menace the empire, and while Caesar and Lepidus fight to preserve their dominions, Antony, famed throughout the world as a brave and noble soldier, dallies in Egypt, bewitched by the charms of the beautiful queen, Cleopatra. When messengers arrive from Caesar asking for help in the wars, Antony refuses to see them. His love for Cleopatra has robbed him of any sense of duty. He embraces her, saying:

> Let Rome in Tiber melt, and the wide arch
> Of the ranged empire fall! Here is my space.
> Kingdoms are clay; our dungy earth alike
> Feed beast as man: the nobleness of life
> Is to do thus.

There is a brief reconciliation as, hearing of his wife's death, Antony returns to Rome and marries Caesar's sister. But his love for Cleopatra draws him back. Enobarbus, Antony's closest friend, knows the power of her hold over his captain and comments, "He will to his Egyptian dish again." But Enobarbus is not immune to Cleopatra's irresistible charm, made even more seductive in its opulent Eastern setting. He tells us that Antony saw Cleopatra for the first time in her barge on the river Cydnus. Her beauty, he says, "beggar'd all description," and at dinner that night Antony "pays his heart / For what his eyes eat only." Nor, he says, will Antony ever tire of her:

> Age cannot wither her, nor custom stale
> her infinite variety; other women cloy
> The appetites they feed; but she makes hungry
> Where most she satisfies: for vilest things
> Become themselves in her; that the holy priests
> Bless her when she is riggish.

Caesar, incensed by Antony's treatment of his sister, loses patience and takes control. He defeats Pompey, imprisons Lepidus, and leads his forces against Antony. Although Cleopatra offers her help, everyone in Antony's camp knows that Caesar has a stronger and more experienced fleet. But even Antony's generalship has deserted him and he foolishly decides to fight the battle at sea. When the outcome of the battle of Actium is still undecided, Cleopatra turns fearfully for home and Antony follows her. He suffers a crushing defeat. His anger with Cleopatra is soothed by her tears. But in the battle for Alexandria, her fleet once more deserts him and Cleopatra, in the face of his anger, escapes to her monument.

Cleopatra sends a messenger to Antony to say she has slain herself. In one dramatic line—a masterly use of monosyllables—Shakespeare reveals Antony's grief: "the long day's task is done, / And we must sleep." Cleopatra was his "day o'all the world," and without her he does not want to go on living. He resolves to kill himself, "a Roman by a Roman / Valiantly vanquisht," confident he will be reunited with her "where souls do couch on flowers." He falls on his sword and is carried, mortally wounded, to Cleopatra to die in her arms. In the magnificent final scene Cleopatra rises to true greatness as, calling Antony husband, she poisons herself with the bite of an asp. She goes proudly to meet her Antony, to claim "that kiss / Which is my heaven to have."

There is a sense of fulfilment at the end of *Antony and Cleopatra* that foreshadows the romances that Shakespeare was still to write. Both lovers counted the world well lost for a kiss, and such love as theirs could end only as it did. In the circumstances, I feel that neither of them would have wished it otherwise.

But although Shakespeare wrote so glowingly about Antony, a man to whom "realms and islands were / As plates dropt from his pocket," he ordered his own affairs very differently. Images from the English countryside find their way into Cleopatra's Egypt, suggesting he may have written some of the play at home in Stratford. The enchanting queen flees from the battle of Actium as if plagued by flies, "the breese upon her, like a cow in June," and Antony pursues her "like a doting mallard." Shakespeare's thoughts were never far from his native Warwickshire and Stratford. His family and friends were there and he could afford to spend more time with them. He had owned New Place, in the heart of the town, for ten years. It was one of the finest houses in Stratford, with five bays, a courtyard, and barns. Behind the house was a large garden, an asset which must have delighted Shakespeare, with his love of flowers and the wildlife they attract. (Except caterpillars! Their depredations are a frequent source of imagery in his plays.) The house needed some repairs and he evidently bought too much stone, as Stratford Corporation bought the surplus from him. He also enlarged the garden. He would need help in so large a garden, and in 1602 he acquired the copyhold of a cottage

Our path to the obelisk in Welcombe Hills and Clopton Country Park

opposite New Place, possibly to house a gardener.

Shakespeare certainly would have been back in his hometown in June 1607 for the marriage of his witty and intelligent elder daughter, Susanna, to a local physician, John Hall. He would have approved of the marriage, as her husband was much respected and took her to a comfortable home, Hall's Croft, in the Old Town area of Stratford close to Holy Trinity Church. The following February he probably stood proudly by the font as his grandchild, Elizabeth, was christened. These mellowing influences in his life must have contributed to the sweet-natured heroines he was to depict in his romances. But later in the year, in September, he would return to Stratford again, this time with a heavy heart, for the funeral of his mother.

Home in Stratford, we can imagine Shakespeare, now a wealthy man, walking in the surrounding countryside, enjoying its beauty, certainly, but also with an eye for a shrewd investment. Northeast of the town, the hamlet of Welcombe gave its name to a large open field, to the west of which were the hamlets and open fields of Old Stratford and Bishopton. In May 1602 Shakespeare bought a freehold estate of 127 acres around Old Stratford. Three years later he paid £440 (a very large sum of money in those days) for a thirty-one year lease of part of the tithes—the profits from a tenth part of a crop originally claimed by the church—payable for the corn and hay produced in the fields of "Stratforde, Olde Stratforde, Welcombe and Bishopton." The tithes had been confiscated from the church at the Reformation, passing into lay hands. Although he was thrifty, there is no hint that Shakespeare was ever mean. Ben Jonson, who could be critical of Shakespeare's work but never of the man, writes, "he was indeed honest and of an open and free nature."

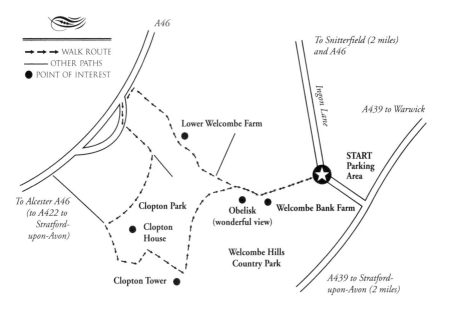

I n this walk, we return with Shakespeare to Stratford to
ramble in the **Welcombe Hills.** They are little changed
since he walked in this lovely countryside so close to
his home. The area is now preserved as the **Welcombe
Hills and Clopton Country Park** and is open for all to
enjoy. The walk starts from the car park beside Ingon Lane
at the eastern entrance to the reserve. Following the
bridleway sign, walk up the drive towards Welcombe Bank
Cottage and Farm. The obelisk you see beyond the farm
was erected in 1876 by Robert Needham Philips, a
"Merchant and manufacturer," in memory of his elder
brother, Mark Philips. Pass the farm on your left and go
through a gate. Here, we turn right to follow a sunken
grassy path leading past a white-walled cottage on your
right. But first climb up to the obelisk to stand where
Shakespeare must often have stood and enjoy, as he did, a

Clopton House, where conspirators met to plan the destruction of the Houses of Parliament in the infamous Gunpowder Plot

splendid **view over Stratford** and the rich fields of the Feldon to Edgehill and the Cotswolds. In *King Lear*, Shakespeare could be describing his native landscape as the aging king grants a share of his lands to his daughter Goneril:

> With shadowy forests and with champains [fertile land] richt
> With plenteous rivers and wide-skirted meads.

The vast, many-chimneyed mansion in the deep hollow on your right was built as a private residence by Mark Philips and is now a hotel. Return to the path past the cottage and continue heading north to go through a gate. Ignore a bridleway sign on your left and keep straight on uphill. At the top of the hill, keep ahead through a gate along a grassy path. Today the fields on either side are hedged and provide grazing for sheep. When Shakespeare walked this way, he would have crossed a great open field sown with arable crops, but already he would have heard threats of enclosure from William Combe, a large landowner in Welcombe.

The path curves right, then left, to continue heading north, running downhill past Lower Welcombe Farm. Then it leads uphill to bring you through tall gates to the A46. Turn left along the wide path beside the road, then follow the lane to the left of the main road for about a quarter-mile. As the lane begins to curve right downhill, bear left off the corner, following the footpath signed for Stratford. The path runs high beside a hedge on the left, with more splendid **views over the Avon valley** on your right. Continue for about a quarter-mile until you come to a wooden gate. Turn right just before the gate, with a hedge on your left and open fields on your right. The path descends into a hollow, and you will see a small iron gate on your left. Go through the gate and turn right to resume your original heading. Now you are walking though another part of the reserve, the parkland surrounding **Clopton House.** Walk down the valley, going through three gates, until you come to a wide crosstrack bordered by fine chestnut trees. Turn left and follow the tree-shaded track through a gate. Bear half-right diagonally over the grass towards a row of houses, and go through a gate opening to a narrow footpath. Turn left to follow the path, with the houses on your right and the parkland on your left. Over the parkland you will see Clopton House, which dates from the sixteenth century. This fine manor house was the family home of the Clopton family, lords of the manor from the thirteenth to the eighteenth centuries. At Michaelmas 1605, perhaps while Shakespeare was tending his garden at New Place, Clopton House was rented by Ambrose Rookwood, one of the conspirators involved in the Gunpowder Plot. Imagine the stir this must have

The beautiful chestnut tree avenue in Clopton Park.

caused in Stratford when news of the plot hit the headlines!

After about 150 yards, you come to a bridleway sign by a gate on the left. Turn left through the gate and keep ahead to go through another gate. Turn right to walk along a broad avenue bordered by more chestnut trees. This brings you through a gate to **Clopton Tower,** now a private residence. Pass the tower on your right and turn left uphill. The asphalt track gives way to a pleasant footpath that winds uphill through the wooded glades of the country park. Keep a fence on your left as you near the top of the hill, then bear right towards the obelisk, still keeping the fence on your left. Go through a gate on your left to join the path you followed earlier in the walk, and turn right to retrace your steps through a gate, passing the obelisk on your right. Turn left past Welcombe Bank Farm to return to your car.

A delightful corner of Clopton Park

Starting point and parking
The parking area off Ingon Lane where we start this walk is marked with a car park sign on the Ordnance Survey Explorer map but at present is not signed off the road. Leave Stratford along the A439, and after about 2 miles turn left for Snitterfield along Ingon Lane. The parking area is about one-half mile further on your left. GR 215 572.

Public transport
To travel from Stratford, take the bus for Snitterfield via Ingon Lane and ask to alight at the entrance to the Welcombe Hills and Clopton Country Park (Welcombe Bank Farm). For times, contact Welcombe Garages at (01789) 204393.

Length of walk: 3.5 miles.

Map: Ordnance Survey Explorer Map No. 205.

F rom the parking area, follow the drive past Welcombe Bank Farm, through a gate. Turn right (visit obelisk), then continue past a cottage, through the next gate. Keep ahead uphill, then follow the path downhill past Lower Welcombe Farm and uphill again to A46. Turn left along the lane to the left of the main road for about a quarter-mile, then turn left along the footpath signed for Stratford. After about a quarter-mile, just before a wooden gate, turn right and follow the path (hedge on your left) downhill to go through a small gate on the left. Bear right through three gates to a crosstrack. Turn left to continue through a gate. Bear half-right diagonally over the field and go through a gate to a narrow footpath. Turn left to a bridleway on the left. Take this over the field to an avenue. Turn right to Clopton Tower. Turn left and climb the hill, keeping a fence on your left. As you reach the top, bear right towards the obelisk, still with a fence on your left, to a gate opening to the track followed earlier in the walk. Bear right through the gate to retrace your steps to your car.

CHAPTER 11

GOLDEN DAYS BESIDE THE AVON

With fairest flowers
Whilst summer lasts, and I live here, Fidele,
I'll sweeten thy sad grave: thou shalt not lack
The flower that's like thy face, pale primrose; nor
The azured harebell, like thy veins; no, nor
The leaf of eglantine, whom not to slander
Out-sweeten'd not thy breath. . . .

—Arviragus, *Cymbeline*

After 1607 Shakespeare wrote just three more plays on his own: *Cymbeline*, *The Winter's Tale* and *The Tempest*. He worked with other writers on four plays, *Pericles*, *Henry VIII*, *The Two Noble Kinsmen* and *Cardenio*. References to *Cardenio* prove some of the play was his work, but the play itself has been lost. New Place, his family, and friends were taking up more of his time, and it is likely that around 1610 he left his lodgings in London to retire to Stratford. But before he retired, an exciting new prospect had opened up, for him and the King's Men.

James Burbage had obtained the lease on part of the former Blackfriars Priory in 1596 and fitted up a theater, only for the company to find itself banned by local protesters from using it. In 1608 his sons, Cuthbert and Richard, recovered the lease and this time there were no protests. But the same month a severe outbreak of the plague closed all the theaters. The King's Men had to wait until they reopened late in 1609 before they could use Blackfriars. Richard Burbage formed a new company of owners, or "housekeepers," including Shakespeare. We can imagine Shakespeare and the rest of the company as they admired their new indoor theater, busily discussing the opportunities it would present. The roofed theater was warm and comfortable, so audience numbers would no longer be affected by the weather. It was well-lit by candelabra and lanterns, so plays could be performed in the evening as well as in the afternoon. Theatrical effects such as ghostly apparitions could be more easily achieved. Music, popular with all classes of society, could play a much greater part in their productions.

Tastes in entertainment were changing. Elaborate productions known as masques, which combined lyrics with music and dancing, were becoming increasingly popular at court. The best were being written by Shakespeare's friend and rival Ben Jonson, with lavish settings devised by Inigo

Jones. They included magnificent rituals intended to amaze and transport the audience. Plays with long rhetorical speeches and a succession of battle scenes were not as effective at Blackfriars, patronized by residents from an aristocratic area of London, as they were at the Globe. Shakespeare had new challenges and new audiences to please. These presented no problems to our greatest playwright. He turned from tragedy, history, and comedy to write his romances, combining elements from all three.

Cymbeline was completed in 1610. With its magical atmosphere, variety of scene, and romantic theme, it was admirably suited to the times. To the accompaniment of solemn music, a masque is introduced into the play in the course of which "Jupiter descends in thunder and lightning sitting upon an eagle"—an effect which would be difficult to achieve in any theater, especially on a sunny afternoon at the Globe! The play contains one of his loveliest songs, the *Dirge for Fidele*, part of which I quote at the beginning of this chapter. Like *The Winter's Tale* (discussed in chapter 5), *Cymbeline* is a dreamlike story with many of the qualities of a fairytale. Shakespeare weaves elements of tragedy and comedy into the fanciful plot and sets them against a historical background. But the old master still has a great deal to say. It is a play with a message. Underlying the action are deeply religious values: sin and repentance, forgiveness and reconciliation. There is no looking back to the medieval world of the mystery and morality plays. Shakespeare sets these themes in his own times, colored by the ideas of the Renaissance. But many in his audience would still see Jupiter in the same light as the early humanist scholars, as an allegorical figure representing Christ.

Imogen, the daughter of Cymbeline, King of Britain, is one of Shakespeare's most delightful heroines—loyal, spirited and brave. She has secretly married an orphan,

Posthumus, a gentleman brought up at court. The king's second wife, a wicked woman skilled in distilling poisons, wishes Imogen to marry Cloten, her foolish son by a previous marriage. Imogen is spurned by her father but stays faithful to Posthumus, who is banished to Rome. There he meets Iachimo, who makes a wager with him. After just one meeting, Iachimo tells Posthumus, he will bring back proof he has seduced Imogen. Iachimo travels to Britain, and when no lies can convince Imogen that Posthumus has other lovers, he gains access to her bedroom by trickery while she is asleep.

Iachimo makes no attempt to seduce her, but notes details of her room. He takes a bracelet that Posthumus had given her off her arm and sees she has a mole on her left breast. In the light of such proof, Posthumus is convinced Imogen has yielded to Iachimo and in his fury writes to Imogen to meet him at Milford Haven. He instructs his servant Pisanio to accompany her and murder her on the way. Pisanio, sure of her innocence, persuades Imogen to disguise herself as a boy and join Lucius, a Roman general who is invading Britain. Lost in the mountains, Imogen, who now calls herself Fidele, meets the banished lord Belarius and two young men whom he says are his sons. Although she is unaware of the fact, they are her brothers, stolen by Belarius from the palace as babies and brought up by him in his refuge, a mountain cave. Cloten, dressed in clothes once worn by Posthumus, follows Imogen, is killed by the brothers, and is beheaded. Imogen, feeling ill, takes a drug that makes her appear to be dead. She revives and, mistaking the headless body of Cloten for Posthumus, joins Lucius. In the following battle, the bravery of Belarius, his two supposed sons, and Posthumus helps to win victory for Cymbeline. They are all brought before him. The truth is revealed, Iachimo confesses and is pardoned, and Belarius is also forgiven. Cymbeline realizes

Holy Trinity Church seen from across the river Avon

his folly. He is reunited with Imogen, and Posthumus and his two lost sons are returned to him. On this note of reconciliation and the promise of future happiness, the play ends.

There is plenty here to please all who love fairy tales! But the play convinces because we recognize the characters as real people not afraid to show their feelings. Cymbeline does not mince his words. In his fury, he calls his daughter "a vile thing" and commands the queen to take her away "and pen her up." Convinced of Imogen's faithlessness, Posthumus condemns all women in a speech that could have been spoken by Othello:

> For there's no motion
> That tends to vice in man, but I affirm
> It is the woman's part: be it lying, note it,
> The woman's; flattering, hers; deceiving, hers;
> Lust and rank thoughts, hers, hers. . . .

Imogen is all too human. Feeling vulnerable and nervous, she is driven by hunger to enter the cave of Belarius, drawing her sword in the hope that any enemy will be as frightened of it as she is.

Iachimo wants to win his wager and is prepared to slander Imogen to achieve it, but he is not entirely a villain. In her bedchamber, he is allowed to praise her beauty in glorious verse:

> the flame o'the taper
> Bows towards her; and would under-peep her lids,
> To see the enclosed lights, now canopied
> Under these windows, white and azure, laced
> With blue of heaven's own tinct. . . .

As Shakespeare prepared to settle in his Stratford home, he must have reflected, like Belarius:

> O, this life
> Is nobler than attending for a check,
> Richer than doing nothing for a bribe,
> Prouder than rustling in unpaid-for silk.

Perhaps, as he had more time, he revisited some of his favorite haunts in the Cotswolds. The mole on Imogen's left breast is "cinque-spotted, like the crimson drops / I'the bottom of a cowslip." Cowslips are a flower of the chalk downland and flourish in the Cotswold Hills.

After writing *The Winter's Tale*, so reminiscent of the Cotswolds, Shakespeare completed his last romance, *The Tempest*, in 1611. He probably wrote these later plays at home in Stratford, as the stage directions are more detailed. In London, he would have been able to direct his actors verbally.

Again, after evil-doing, repentance brings forgiveness,

reconciliation, and happiness. But in other respects *The Tempest*, the last play Shakespeare wrote on his own, is very different. I suggest that Shakespeare, with perhaps a twinkle in his eye, wished to prove to his rival Ben Jonson that, should he feel inclined, he could write a great masque too! As the action is dominated by an all-controlling magical presence, there is no clash of individual wills and little conflict or suspense. *The Tempest* is a gorgeous musical spectacle.

The action takes place on a mythical island in the Mediterranean. All that happens there is governed by the supernatural power of Prospero, the exiled Duke of Milan. Those who arrive on the island's shore do so at his command and become subject to his will. In this respect he could be compared to Oberon in *A Midsummer Night's Dream*. But the characters in *The Tempest* are not as recognizably human as some of those we encounter in Oberon's forest. Can the drunken butler and jester shipwrecked on Prospero's island be compared with magnificent "bully Bottom" and his workmates rehearsing their play in the forest on that moonlit midsummer night?

Prospero is living in a cave with his daughter, Miranda, waited on by the island's only other inhabitants: Caliban, a half-beast, half-man monster, and his opposite, the delicate spirit Ariel. Twelve years previously Prospero's brother, Antonio, allied with Alonso, King of Naples, had usurped his dukedom and cast him away at sea with Miranda, then just three years old. After landing on the island, the studious Prospero developed his magical power. Now he is seeking revenge. The play opens with a violent storm raised by Prospero to wreck the ship carrying Antonio, Alonso, Alonso's brother Sebastian, and Alonso's son Ferdinand (an admirable young man who Prospero feels would make an ideal husband for Miranda). They all arrive on the island. Ferdinand lands separately, sees Miranda, and without much ado they fall in love.

Apart from Ferdinand and an old councillor, Gonzago, who had been faithful to Prospero, the castaways bring their evil with them. Sebastian and Antonio are about to murder Alonso and Gonzago, but Ariel is sent by his master to prevent this. Caliban, who hates Prospero, leads two drunken members of the shipwrecked crew to his cave intending to murder him. But all are under Prospero's power, and after he has ordered Ariel to drive his enemies almost distracted, they become his helpless prisoners. When they repent, Prospero forgives them:

> The rarer action is
> In virtue than in vengeance: they being penitent,
> The sole drift of my purpose doth extend
> Not a frown further. . . .

Caliban is also thwarted and comes to realize how foolish he has been. Prospero commands Ariel to entertain the young lovers with a masque. Their future union is blessed by classical goddesses in words and song, and reapers "properly habited . . . join with the nymphs in a graceful dance." This is a masque within a masque! Throughout the play, there is music, the key element in these sumptuous entertainments. Ariel sings Shakespeare's loveliest songs, and Ferdinand's grief for the father he believes dead is soothed by music, which he says "crept by me upon the water, / Allaying both their fury and my passion / With its sweet air." Music is ever-present. "The isle is full of noises," says Caliban, "Sounds and sweet airs, that give delight and hurt not."

After this final service for Prospero, Ariel is freed. With his former enemies reconciled and Miranda about to be married to Ferdinand, Prospero can sail happily back to Milan to reclaim his dukedom. To the accompaniment of solemn music, he renounces his magical powers:

> But this rough magic
> I here abjure....
>
> . . . .
>   I'll break my staff,
> Bury it certain fathoms in the earth,
> And deeper than did ever plummet sound
> I'll drown my book.

Shakespeare, who held audiences spellbound for over twenty years, is ready to leave the stage. He would collaborate with some of the rising generation of playwrights if they wished. He had said his say, exploring our human predicament to the full. To paraphrase Charles Reade, he has made us laugh and made us cry. Now his family, New Place with its garden, and the Warwickshire countryside, all of which had never been far from his thoughts, awaited him.

He was soon caught up in Stratford affairs. In 1611 he joined with the aldermen and other important members of the community to contribute towards forwarding a bill in Parliament to repair the highways. He would have had some muddy rides as he travelled back and forth to London! He still had an eye for a good investment, and in March 1613 he returned to London to sign the deeds to buy the gatehouse at Blackfriars, close to the theater. The indenture was also signed by John Heminge, John Jackson, and William Johnson. The house was close to Puddle Dock, from where Shakespeare must often have taken the ferry across the river to Bankside and the Globe theater. But now he saw the gatehouse solely as an investment, and the next day it was mortgaged to the seller.

Shakespeare must have been alarmed and worried when, during a performance of *Henry VIII* on June 29,

1613, a cannon shot set the thatched roof of the Globe alight and the building was burned to the ground. No one was injured—one spectator's breeches were set on fire, but he doused the flames with "bottle ale"—and the theater was speedily rebuilt.

It is pleasant to think of Shakespeare at home enjoying his library and his garden. His plays reveal his delight in flowers for their scent and beauty, and herbs for their use in cookery and medicine. New plants were being introduced from America and the Canary Islands, and after James I attempted to develop the silk industry by encouraging English gardeners to grow mulberry trees, Shakespeare planted one at New Place. But it is the wildflowers blooming beside the river and in the woods and fields around Stratford that he celebrates in his loveliest poetry. In *The Winter's Tale*, Perdita offers her guests

> daffodils,
> That come before the swallow dares, and take
> The winds of March with beauty; violets dim,
> But sweeter than the lids of Juno's eyes.

And he now had time to enjoy the company of his friends and welcome guests. John Aubrey records he was "very good company," and at Christmas 1614 he entertained a preacher at New Place with "one quart of sack and one quart of claret wine." I see no reason to doubt Nicholas Rowe's comment in his short *Life of Mr. William Shakespear*, written towards the end of the seventeenth century, that "The latter part of his Life was spent . . . in Ease, Retirement, and the Conversation of his friends..."

On February 10, 1616, his daughter Judith married Thomas Quiney, the son of neighbors. The previous month Shakespeare had made his will. On March 25, after Judith's marriage, he made a second draft describing himself as "in perfect health and memory, God be praised." His wife, Anne, would be provided for, as she had her right of dower—her widow's third portion—and the assurance of a home either at New Place or with Susanna at Hall's Croft. It is possible he did not approve of Judith's marriage which, having taken place during the prohibited period before Easter, resulted in Judith and Thomas being excommunicated by the Consistory Court at Worcester. So he left most of his property and investments to Susanna and her husband, perhaps hoping she would have a son. He was not to know Susanna would have no more children. Other small bequests included money to buy mourning rings for his old actor friends John Heminge, Richard Burbage, and Henry Condell. Heminge and Condell were to repay his friendship when they painstakingly put together the First Folio of his plays, published in 1623. No hurt was intended when he mentions leaving Anne his second best bed. Beds and their draperies were highly valued items in the Elizabethan household and this was possibly an heirloom she had brought from her home when they were married. The best bed was always reserved for guests. In spite of long absences, a certain Dark Lady, and possibly other hiccups along the way, their marriage had lasted, and I believe he was happy with Anne in retirement. Perhaps quoting his own Christopher Sly in *The Taming of the Shrew*, he had said to her:

> *Come, madam wife, sit by my side,*
> *and let the world slip: we shall ne'er be younger.*

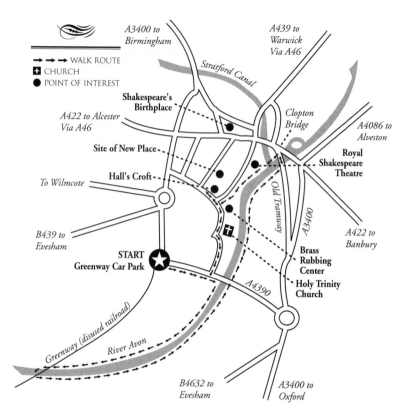

→ → → WALK ROUTE
✚ CHURCH
● POINT OF INTEREST

A3400 to
Birmingham

A439 to
Warwick
Via A46

Stratford Canal

Shakespeare's
Birthplace

A422 to Alcester
Via A46

Clopton
Bridge

A4086 to
Alveston

Site of New Place

Royal
Shakespeare
Theatre

Hall's Croft

To Wilmcote

Old Tramway

A3400

B439 to
Evesham

A422 to
Banbury

START
Greenway Car Park

Brass
Rubbing
Center

Holy Trinity
Church

A4390

Greenway (disused railroad)

River Avon

B4632 to
Evesham

A3400 to
Oxford

P erhaps Shakespeare rambled with Anne along the
pleasant paths beside the Avon only a few minutes
away from New Place. The route of this walk follows
them along riverside paths they must have known. Our
starting point is the Greenway Car Park off the A4390,
southwest of the Stratford town center. To start the walk,
face the car park entrance and turn right to follow the
hedged footpath running through the trees to the right of
the main road. In a little over a quarter mile, you come to
the **bank of the Avon.** Turn right to follow the footpath
beside the river, which is on your left. The river flows
swiftly, fringed by the drooping boughs of willow trees, a
scene which Shakespeare must have had in mind when he

wrote Queen Gertrude's account of Ophelia's drowning in *Hamlet*:

> There is a willow grows aslant a brook,
> That shows his hoar leaves in the glassy stream;
> There with fantastic garlands did she come.

With his wonderful ability to choose just the right word, Shakespeare is able to capture the sound and movement of the river as well as its appearance. In *Two Gentlemen of Verona*, he writes:

> The current that, with gentle murmur glides,
> Thou know'st, being stopped, impatiently doth rage;
> But when his fair course is not hindered,
> He makes sweet music with the enamell'd stones,
> Giving a gentle kiss to every sedge
> He overtaketh in his pilgrimage;
> And so by many winding nooks he strays,
> With willing sport, to the wild ocean.

The wildlife of the river provides Shakespeare with some delightful images. In *Venus and Adonis*, the reluctant Adonis is compared to

> a dive-dapper, peering through a wave,
> Who being looked on, ducks as quickly in.

And Shakespeare obviously enjoyed fishing. Ursula tells Hero in *Much Ado About Nothing*:

> The pleasant'st angling is to see the fish
> Cut with her golden oars the silver stream
> And greedily devour the treacherous bait.

Susanna Shakespeare's married home, Hall's Croft, seen from the garden.

After about 1.25 miles, just before you come to a former railway bridge over the river, go through a gate and pass a picnic area. Take the path on the right, which climbs to the track of the disused railway (now a footpath), and turn left to cross the bridge. Keep ahead for about 50 yards, then turn left down a footpath leading through a gate. Turn left to go through another gate, and bear right to join the path along the south bank of the river. Follow the well-signed path through all gates and up and down steps for about 1.5 miles. At times the path runs along the top of a **wooded cliff** sloping down to the water's edge. The path leads under the A4390 and continues beside the river, with the Stratford recreation ground on your right. You pass two locks, and there is a **fine view over the river** to Holy Trinity Church and shortly afterwards the Royal Shakespeare Theatre.

The path curves right, past Stratford Boat Club. Turn left to cross the brick-built tramway bridge. (The bridge was part of the old railway connecting Stratford with Moreton-in-Marsh that carried freight in horse-drawn trucks during the nineteenth century.) Just past Cox's Yard, turn left to walk past the **rose garden** and cross the canal bridge to follow the riverside. Continue along the terrace of the **Royal Shakespeare Theatre** and follow the path through the **theater gardens** to the pillared building housing a Brass Rubbing Centre. Turn right around the Centre, leaving it on your right, towards the wall of the garden, then turn left to go through a gateway to the road in the Old Town area of Stratford opposite Holy Trinity Parish Centre.

Turn right to visit **Hall's Croft,** the comfortable home of Shakespeare's daughter Susanna, who married highly-respected local physician John Hall in 1607. It is a fascinating house appropriately furnished and decorated with many sixteenth- and seventeenth-century paintings. The kitchen has an enormous fireplace equipped with a spit for roasting and a drip tray. One room is furnished as a seventeenth-century doctor's surgery. An exhibition gives details of Doctor Hall's life and his cures, which were based mainly on herbs. The garden includes a formal herb bed growing many of the herbs the doctor mentions in his casebooks.

After visiting the house, turn left to walk down the churchway to follow Shakespeare to his last resting place, Stratford's beautiful **Church of the Holy Trinity.** Shakespeare died on St. George's Day, April 23, 1616. As a "lay rector," or tithe holder, he was entitled to be buried in the church. He was fifty-two, a good age for his time. On April 25, his body was interred in the chancel in front of the high altar. When Anne died seven years later, she asked to be buried with him, and she lies on his left. On the chancel wall above his grave, a bust of Shakespeare looks benignly down on the thousands of visitors who come

The Royal Shakespeare Theatre beside the Avon

to honor England's greatest poet.

Tributes to Shakespeare have been paid by many eminent people, but the greatest tribute is one we can all pay. It is simply to enjoy his work. To quote Rosalind at the conclusion of *As You Like It*, Shakespeare's hope was always "that the play may please."

Turn left from the church to follow Mill Lane past Lucy's Mill. This leads to a narrow footpath running under the A4390 to meet the path from the Greenway Car Park you took at the start of the walk. Turn right to retrace your steps to your car.

The river Avon

Starting point
Greenway Car Park off the A4390. GR 197 540. To avoid the Stratford town center, turn left off the A422 along the A3400. At the roundabout, turn right along the A4390, which crosses the river to the Greenway Car Park, signed to the left of the next roundabout. If you have no car, as the walk is circular, you could begin the walk by the river at any point and ignore the access details to and from the car park.

Length of walk: 4 miles.

Map: Ordnance Survey Explorer Map No 205.

The Royal Shakespeare Company has a ticket hotline: telephone (0870) 609 1110. You can also book online (*www.rsc.org.uk*) or in person. The theater foyer box office is open from 9.30 AM to 8 PM Monday through Saturday (6 PM when there is no evening performance). Tours of the Royal Shakespeare and Swan theaters are available most days; telephone (01789) 403405.

Hall's Croft is one of the properties owned by the Shakespeare Birthplace Trust. For details of opening times and admission charges, telephone (01789) 292102 or visit the Trust's official website: *www.shakespeare.org.uk*.

The website for Holy Trinity Church is *www.stratford-upon-avon.org*.

F ace the entrance to the Greenway Car Park, and turn right along the hedged footpath running to the right of the A4390 to the bank of the Avon. Turn right (river on left), and continue for about 1.25 miles to a path on the right climbing to the track of the disused railway. Turn left to cross the bridge, and after about 50 yards take the path on the left to descend to a gate. Go through the gate, turn left through another gate, and follow the path along the other side of the river to go under the A4390, passing the recreation ground to the tramway bridge. Cross the bridge, turn left just past Cox's Yard, cross the canal bridge and walk along the terrace of the Royal Shakespeare Theatre. Follow the path through gardens to the Brass Rubbing Centre. Turn right, leaving the Centre on your right, then left to leave the gardens and enter the road in the Old Town area of Stratford opposite the Holy Trinity Parish Centre. Turn right to visit Hall's Croft, then left to Holy Trinity Church. Turn left from the church entrance along Mill Lane and continue along the footpath under the A4390 and turn right to return to the Greenway Car Park.

WALKING IN
ENGLAND

E ngland is a marvellous country for the walker.
Crammed into this small island is an amazing variety
of scenery and wildlife. History lies round every
corner. You will find something of interest on even the
shortest walk. All land is owned, of course, but England has
a splendid network of public rights-of-way. These are
ancient paths that people have followed over the
centuries—to market, to church, to visit friends in the next
village, or to the nearest pub—now carefully recorded on
definitive maps and open for everyone to enjoy. They are
usually signed off roads or car parks with finger boards that
indicate whether they are footpaths for pedestrians only or
bridleways for pedestrians and horse riders. Look for yellow
arrows or blobs on fences, stiles or trees to indicate
footpaths, and blue markings for bridleways. Sometimes old
roads have now become public paths and may be signed as
byways.

Ordnance Survey®, the government agency responsible
for English mapping, publishes a range of maps. The best
maps for walkers are the Explorer™ series at 1:25,000 (4
centimeters to 1 kilometer, or 2.5 inches to 1 mile). They
are packed with useful information and show all rights-of-
way. With such a large scale, you may need several, and

A footpath sign and stile

you may prefer the smaller-scale Landranger® series at 1:50,000. Footpaths on the Explorer maps are marked in green dots; bridleways are marked in green dashes. Long distance rights-of-way, usually called trails, are marked in green with small green diamonds at 1-centimeter intervals. On the Landranger maps, footpaths are marked with red dots and bridleways with red dashes.

There are also "permissive paths." These cross private land to which the landowner has granted temporary access. There should be a notice giving permission at the approach to these areas, sometimes accompanied by a map. This permission can be withdrawn at any time and it is wiser to keep to established rights-of-way.

In September 2004 a new law was passed allowing everyone the "right to roam." This gives "open access" to certain areas of private land, usually moors, downland, commons and some open countryside. It is an exciting development and new maps have been drawn up by order of the Countryside Agency to show these areas. However, there are serious drawbacks. Landowners have the right to close the land for twenty-eight days a year and can also restrict access at other times for a variety of reasons. Closure dates are unspecified and could lead to disappointment and problems for walkers. Again, I recommend you keep to established rights-of-way.

Some of the most beautiful areas of the country are owned by the National Trust and generally you are free to roam on its land, although it is always wise to follow a footpath if there is one. The National Trust also owns many of England's most historic homes and gardens, open to the public and always worth a visit. Look for the initials NT or oak leaf logo on the maps. Other properties, also open, may be owned by English Heritage. Some family homes are open for visitors and all details can be obtained from tourist offices. The Forestry Commission allows public access to most of its land.

Ordnance Survey has devised a very useful system to help you find any given point on its maps. Each map has an overlay forming a grid of numbered horizontal and vertical lines. By using this grid, you are guided to the place you wish to find. In this book the starting point for each walk is followed by the letters GR—which stands for Grid Reference—and two groups of numbers. You will find details on how to use the grid system on the Ordnance Survey maps.

Although the authorities do their best, footpaths do get overgrown and even blocked at times. The beginning of a footpath or bridleway may be clearly marked, but then signs may reappear only occasionally. You may find a right-of-way has been rerouted, perhaps after the map or guidebook you are using (including this one!) was printed. If this is a recent change, there should be a map nearby indicating the new route. I hope the directions I give in this book will help you to avoid any difficulties. All my routes follow public rights-of-way, but I cannot be held responsible for any changes and inaccuracies in the text resulting from diversion orders, nor any damage which might be the result of trespassing on private property!

England's lovely green landscape would not be the same without plentiful supplies of rain, and paths can be muddy and slippery. So wear strong shoes—boots, if possible, in stony country—even if you do not intend to walk far. Be careful crossing stiles, they can be shaky. A last word—and the most important! There is a magic symbol on maps: a large blue tankard indicates a pub. Most now serve excellent, reasonably priced meals and snacks as well as drinks. Happy walking!

BIBLIOGRAPHY

There is an enormous number of books about Shakespeare's
life, work and times and it is difficult to give a selection.
I have found the following books most helpful:

Brown, Ivor. *Shakespeare*. (A most enjoyable life containing
    some intriguing theories about Shakespeare's romantic
    entanglements.)
Campbell, S. C. *Only Begotten Sonnets*.
Chambers, Sir Edmund. *William Shakespeare*.
———. *Shakespeare: A Survey*.
Dick, Oliver Lawson, Ed. *Aubrey's Brief Lives*.
Dodd, A. H. *Elizabethan England*.
Emerson, Kathy Lee. *Everyday Life in Elizabethan England*.
Halliday, F. E. *A Shakespeare Companion*. (An indispensable
    guide for all students of Shakespeare.)
———. *The Poetry of Shakespeare's Plays*.
———. *Unfamiliar Shakespeare*.
Holden, Anthony. *William Shakespeare*.
Kermode, Frank. *Shakespeare's Language*.
Piper, David. *The Companion Guide to London*.(Pinpoints
    many places in London with Shakespearian
    connections.)
Prince, F. T. *Shakespeare: The Poems*.
Quennell, Peter. *Shakespeare*.
Rowse, A. L. *William Shakespeare*.
Southworth, John. *Shakespeare The Player*.
Speaight, Robert. *Shakespeare, the Man and his Achievement*.
Spurgeon, Caroline. *Shakespeare's Imagery*.
Trotter, Stewart. *Love's Labour's Found*. (For Shakespeare's
    connection with Titchfield in Hampshire.)

Wilson, J. Dover. *The Essential Shakespeare*
———. *Life in Shakespeare's England.*
Wood, Michael. *In Search of Shakespeare.* (A fascinating approach dealing in depth with the religious problems of the time. I also enjoyed his excellent series on BBC Television.)

INDEX